THE BUREAU OF TRANSPORTATION STATISTICS

PRIORITIES FOR THE FUTURE

CONSTANCE F. CITRO AND JANET L. NORWOOD, *Editors*

Panel on Statistical Programs and Practices of the
Bureau of Transportation Statistics

Committee on National Statistics
Commission on Behavioral and Social Sciences and Education

Transportation Research Board

National Research Council

NATIONAL ACADEMY PRESS
Washington, D.C.   1997

NATIONAL ACADEMY PRESS • 2101 Constitution Avenue, N.W. • Washington, DC 20418

NOTICE: The project that is the subject of this report was approved by the Governing Board of the National Research Council, whose members are drawn from the councils of the National Academy of Sciences, the National Academy of Engineering, and the Institute of Medicine. The members of the committee responsible for the report were chosen for their special competences and with regard for appropriate balance.

This report has been reviewed by a group other than the authors according to procedures approved by a Report Review Committee consisting of members of the National Academy of Sciences, the National Academy of Engineering, and the Institute of Medicine.

This study was supported by contract no. CNST-1-95-06A between the National Academy of Sciences and the Bureau of Transportation Statistics of the U.S. Department of Transportation. Any opinions, findings, conclusions, or recommendations expressed in this publication are those of the author(s) and do not necessarily reflect the view of the organizations or agencies that provided support for this project.

Library of Congress Cataloging Card no.
ISBN 0-309-06404-X

Additional copies available from:

National Academy Press
2101 Constitution Avenue, N.W.
Washington, D.C. 20418

Call 800-624-6242 or 202-334-3313 (in the Washington metropolitan area).
This report is also available on line at http://www.nap.edu

Copyright 1997 by the National Academy of Sciences. All rights reserved.

Printed in the United States of America

PANEL ON STATISTICAL PROGRAMS AND PRACTICES OF THE BUREAU OF TRANSPORTATION STATISTICS

JANET L. NORWOOD (*Chair*), The Urban Institute, Washington, D.C.
VINCENT P. BARABBA, General Motors Corporation, Warren, Michigan
JAMES T. BONNEN, Department of Agricultural Economics, Michigan State University
CAROL S. CARSON, International Monetary Fund, Washington, D.C.
WILLIAM F. EDDY, Department of Statistics, Carnegie Mellon University
EMERSON J. ELLIOTT, National Council for Accreditation of Teacher Education, Washington, D.C.
FRANCIS B. FRANCOIS, American Association of State Highway and Transportation Officials, Washington, D.C.
ROBERT M. GROVES, Joint Program in Survey Methodology, University of Michigan
ROBERT E. MARTINEZ, Secretary of Transportation, Richmond, Virginia
MICHAEL D. MEYER, School of Civil and Environmental Engineering, Georgia Institute of Technology
PETER L. SZANTON, Szanton Associates, Washington, D.C.
CHARLES A. WAITE, CBW Consulting, Falls Church, Virginia
JULIAN WOLPERT, Woodrow Wilson School of Public and International Affairs, Princeton University

CONSTANCE F. CITRO, *Study Director*
KAREN R. HUIE, *Project Assistant*
NANCY HUMPHREY, *Senior Program Officer*
MICHELLE RUDDICK, *Research Assistant*
GERALDINE A. TURNER, *Research Assistant*
ALICE J. WATLAND, *Senior Program Officer*

COMMITTEE ON NATIONAL STATISTICS
1996-1997

NORMAN M. BRADBURN (*Chair*), National Opinion Research Center, University of Chicago
JULIE DAVANZO, RAND, Santa Monica, California
WILLIAM F. EDDY, Department of Statistics, Carnegie Mellon University
JOHN F. GEWEKE, Department of Economics, University of Minnesota, Minneapolis
JOEL B. GREENHOUSE, Department of Statistics, Carnegie Mellon University
ERIC A. HANUSHEK, W. Allen Wallis Institute of Political Economy, Department of Economics, University of Rochester
RODERICK J.A. LITTLE, Department of Biostatistics, University of Michigan
CHARLES F. MANSKI, Department of Economics, University of Wisconsin
WILLIAM NORDHAUS, Department of Economics, Yale University
JANET L. NORWOOD, The Urban Institute, Washington, D.C.
EDWARD B. PERRIN, School of Public Health and Community Medicine, University of Washington
PAUL ROSENBAUM, Department of Statistics, Wharton School, University of Pennsylvania
KEITH F. RUST, Westat, Inc., Rockville, Maryland
FRANCISCO J. SAMANIEGO, Division of Statistics, University of California, Davis

MIRON L. STRAF, *Director*

TRANSPORTATION RESEARCH BOARD EXECUTIVE COMMITTEE 1996-1997

DAVID N. WORMLEY (*Chair*), Dean of Engineering, Pennsylvania State University
SHARON D. BANKS (*Vice Chair*), AC Transit, Oakland, California
BRIAN J.L. BERRY, Department of Engineering, University of Texas at Dallas
LILLIAN C. BORRONE, The Port Authority of New York and New Jersey, New York, New York
DAVID G. BURWELL, Rails-to-Trails Conservancy, Washington, D.C.
E. DEAN CARLSON, Kansas Department of Transportation, Topeka, Kansas
JAMES N. DENN, Minnesota Department of Transportation, St. Paul, Minnesota
JOHN W. FISHER, Department of Civil Engineering, Lehigh University
DENNIS J. FITZGERALD, Capital District Transportation Authority, Albany, New York
DAVID R. GOODE, Norfolk Southern Corporation, Norfolk, Virginia
DELON HAMPTON, Delon Hampton & Associates, Washington, D.C.
LESTER A. HOEL, Department of Civil Engineering, University of Virginia
JAMES L. LAMMIE, Parsons Brinckerhoff, Inc., New York, New York
ROBERT E. MARTINEZ, Secretary of Transportation, Richmond, Virginia
BRADLEY L. MALLORY, Secretary of Transportation, Harrisburg, Pennsylvania
MARSHALL W. MOORE, North Dakota Department of Transportation, Bismarck, North Dakota
CRAIG E. PHILIP, Ingram Barge Company, Nashville, Tennessee
ANDREA RINIKER, Port of Seattle, Seattle, Washington
JOHN M. SAMUELS, Consolidated Rail Corporation (Conrail), Philadelphia, Pennsylvania
WAYNE SHACKELFORD, Georgia Department of Transportation, Atlanta, Georgia
LES STERMAN, East-West Gateway Coordinating Council, St. Louis, Missouri
JOSEPH M. SUSSMAN, Department of Civil and Environmental Engineering, Massachusetts Institute of Technology
JAMES W. VAN LOBEN SELS, CALTRANS, Sacramento, California
MARTIN WACHS, University of California Transportation Center, University of California, Berkeley
DAVID L. WINSTEAD, Maryland Department of Transportation, Baltimore/Washington International Airport, Maryland

ROBERT E. SKINNER, JR., *Executive Director*

The National Academy of Sciences is a private, nonprofit, self-perpetuating society of distinguished scholars engaged in scientific and engineering research, dedicated to the furtherance of science and technology and to their use for the general welfare. Upon the authority of the charter granted to it by the Congress in 1863, the Academy has a mandate that requires it to advise the federal government on scientific and technical matters. Dr. Bruce M. Alberts is president of the National Academy of Sciences.

The National Academy of Engineering was established in 1964, under the charter of the National Academy of Sciences, as a parallel organization of outstanding engineers. It is autonomous in its administration and in the selection of its members, sharing with the National Academy of Sciences the responsibility for advising the federal government. The National Academy of Engineering also sponsors engineering programs aimed at meeting national needs, encourages education and research, and recognizes the superior achievements of engineers. Dr. William A. Wulf is president of the National Academy of Engineering.

The Institute of Medicine was established in 1970 by the National Academy of Sciences to secure the services of eminent members of appropriate professions in the examination of policy matters pertaining to the health of the public. The Institute acts under the responsibility given to the National Academy of Sciences by its congressional charter to be an adviser to the federal government and, upon its own initiative, to identify issues of medical care, research, and education. Dr. Kenneth I. Shine is president of the Institute of Medicine.

The National Research Council was organized by the National Academy of Sciences in 1916 to associate the broad community of science and technology with the Academy's purposes of furthering knowledge and advising the federal government. Functioning in accordance with general policies determined by the Academy, the Council has become the principal operating agency of both the National Academy of Sciences and the National Academy of Engineering in providing services to the government, the public, and the scientific and engineering communities. The Council is administered jointly by both Academies and the Institute of Medicine. Dr. Bruce M. Alberts and Dr. William A. Wulf are chairman and vice chairman, respectively, of the National Research Council.

Acknowledgments

The Panel on Statistical Programs and Practices of the Bureau of Transportation Statistics wishes to thank the many people who helped make possible the preparation of this report.

The staff of the Bureau of Transportation Statistics (BTS) was extremely helpful in providing information about all aspects of the agency's work and output, including its programs, services, electronic and printed products, customers, budget, and staffing. We particularly thank BTS director T.R. Lakshmanan for sharing with us his concept of the role of BTS in the U.S. Department of Transportation (USDOT) and, in particular, the contribution that BTS can make to useful analysis of transportation data. We are also very grateful for the assistance of Philip Fulton, associate director for statistical programs and services, who served as the panel's project officer and who responded to our numerous questions and requests for information with alacrity and thoroughness.

There are many other BTS staff members who made informative presentations to the panel or met with panel members and staff to share their knowledge. In particular, we thank Robert Knisely, deputy director; Rolf Schmitt, associate director for transportation studies; Timothy Carmody, director of the Office of Airline Information; Donald Bright, chief, data administration division, Office of Airline Information; Bruce Spear, assistant director for geographic information services; Robert Zarnetske, assistant director for information technology; Kathleen Bradley, customer services program manager, and Carolee Bush, products and services information program manager. We also thank staff of BTS and Ann Lawson and Belinda Bonds of the Bureau of Economic Analysis who provided information on the transportation satellite account.

Panel members and staff obtained valuable information from other USDOT statistical units about their programs, resources, and perspectives. We are grateful to staff of the following units for the time and information they shared with us: the Safety Data Services Division, Office of System Safety, Federal Aviation Administration; the Statistics and Forecast Branch, Office of Aviation Policy and Plans, Federal Aviation Administration; the Office of Highway Information Management, Federal Highway Administration; the Office of Program Guidance, Federal Transit Administration; the Office of Statistical and Economic Analysis, Maritime Administration; and the National Center for Statistics and Analysis, National Highway Traffic Safety Administration.

We thank Mortimer Downey, deputy secretary of transportation, for an informative presentation at the first meeting of our panel. Alan Pisarski, long-time transportation consultant, provided the panel with useful background information on the history of statistical programs in USDOT at the same meeting.

We are grateful to the staff of the American Association of State Highway and Transportation Officials, who provided us with reports of interviews that they conducted with officials in several state transportation departments about their data needs and priorities. (Also participating in these interviews were staff of BTS and the Federal Highway Administration.) We are also grateful to staff in the transportation departments of the states of Maryland, Michigan, Nebraska, New Jersey, and Vermont, who provided information about their participation in the highway data collection programs that are sponsored by the Office of Highway Information Management in the Federal Highway Administration. The Standing Committee on Planning of the American Association of State Highway and Transportation Officials, chaired by panel member Robert Martinez, held several meetings in 1996 to discuss BTS's data products and services, the results of which were shared with us. (This committee includes representatives of most state transportation departments.)

Our panel study was conducted collaboratively by the Committee on National Statistics (CNSTAT) and the Transportation Research Board (TRB), and we benefited from the perspectives of both of these units of the National Research Council. Robert Skinner, executive director of TRB, and Miron Straf, director of CNSTAT, briefed the panel at its first meeting on the developments that led to the request for our panel study.

TRB staff members Nancy Humphrey and Alice Watland provided able assistance to the panel through their active participation in panel meetings and comments on drafts of the panel's report. Nancy Humphrey also assisted the panel by obtaining information from the other modal administrations in USDOT about the scope of their statistical operations, staffing, and resource levels. In addition, she briefed the panel about the TRB study that resulted in the report, *Data for Decisions* (National Research Council, 1992a), which reviewed transportation data needs for national policy making and played a role in the establishment of BTS.

Michelle Ruddick, an intern with CNSTAT, prepared a study of nine federal-state data collection programs, including those of the Federal Highway Administration, which provided the panel with useful perspectives. Geraldine Turner, chief economist of the Virginia Department of Motor Vehicles, provided valuable assistance to panel member Robert Martinez in interviewing staff in the USDOT modal administrations.

The panel is grateful to Christine McShane, editor with the Commission on Behavioral and Social Sciences and Education, for fine editorial work and an eagle eye that contributed to the readability of the report. Karen Huie of the CNSTAT staff was an outstanding project assistant for the panel. She made excellent logistical arrangements for the panel's second, third, and fourth meetings, performed admirably in preparing the final manuscript of the report, and contributed to several of the panel's analyses of BTS products, customers, and staff. Agnes Gaskin also assisted the panel by ably arranging for its first meeting.

The panel is especially indebted to Constance Citro, senior study director with CNSTAT, who had overall responsibility for the project. Her skills in organizing and guiding our deliberations and the knowledge she imparted from her wide experience with many CNSTAT studies were invaluable to us. We were fortunate to have her as study director and to benefit from her talents and experience.

Finally, I want to thank the panel members for their generous contributions of time and expert knowledge. They all participated in one or more working groups that the panel established to consider BTS's budget and staffing, data quality standards, transportation data users, data dissemination technology, federal-state transportation data programs, relationships with other USDOT modal administrations, and relationships with other federal statistical and policy agencies. The working groups undertook a variety of activities, including interviews with USDOT staff and transportation data users, the commissioning of background papers, and the preparation of position statements and issue papers for consideration by the full panel at its lively and productive meetings. Overall, this was an exceptionally hard-working group of people, who conducted a wide-ranging, thorough, and thoughtful assessment of BTS's work to date and priorities for the future. It has been a genuine pleasure to work with them.

JANET L. NORWOOD, *Chair*
Panel on Statistical Programs and Practices
of the Bureau of Transportation Statistics

Contents

EXECUTIVE SUMMARY   1
   The Need for Improved Transportation Statistics, 1
   Assessing BTS, 2
   Reauthorization, 3
   Focusing on Quality, 4
   Ensuring Relevance, 5
   Building an Agency, 7

1 INTRODUCTION   9
   Methods of Study, 10
   The Report, 11
   A Note on Reauthorization Legislation, 12

2 HISTORY AND ASSESSMENT OF BTS   13
   Transportation Data Programs in Historical Perspective, 13
   Assessing BTS, 21
   Recommendation, 30

3 FOCUSING ON DATA QUALITY   31
   Dimensions of Quality, 32
   Staffing, 36
   Quality Standards, 40
   Documenting Data Quality, 46
   Data Evaluation and Improvement, 60
   Recommendations, 62

| 4 | ENSURING RELEVANCE | 64 |

Dimensions of Relevance, 65
A Vision of a Comprehensive Transportation Data System, 66
A BTS Implementation Plan, 68
Ensuring Relevance: Transportation Indicators, 69
Coordination of Data Collection and Filling Gaps, 76
Identifying User Needs, 79
Analysis Programs, 82
Recommendations, 86

| 5 | BUILDING AN AGENCY | 87 |

Ensuring Independence, 88
Building Trust, 91
Attaining Leadership, 97
Recommendations, 98

ACRONYMS USED IN THE REPORT	99
REFERENCES	102
APPENDICES	107

A	THE INTERMODAL SURFACE TRANSPORTATION EFFICIENCY ACT OF 1991: REFERENCES TO THE BUREAU OF TRANSPORTATION STATISTICS	109
B	SELECTED STATISTICAL AGENCIES AND PROGRAMS	116
C	PRINCIPLES AND PRACTICES FOR A FEDERAL STATISTICAL AGENCY: HOW BTS COMPARES	120
D	IMPROVING *NATIONAL TRANSPORTATION STATISTICS:* AIRLINE SAFETY AS A CASE STUDY	126
E	DESCRIPTIONS OF CD-ROM PRODUCTS ON THE BTS WEB SITE	131
F	INTEGRATING DATA AND FILLING GAPS: THE CASE OF HOUSEHOLD TRAVEL	138
G	BIOGRAPHICAL SKETCHES	141

The Bureau of Transportation Statistics

PRIORITIES FOR
THE FUTURE

Executive Summary

The Bureau of Transportation Statistics (BTS) was established in the U.S. Department of Transportation (USDOT) by the 1991 Intermodal Surface Transportation Efficiency Act (ISTEA). The same ISTEA legislation also mandated that the National Academy of Sciences/National Research Council review the statistical programs and practices of BTS to improve the relevance and quality of transportation data. Topics identified for study include the role of BTS in providing statistical leadership in USDOT and its relationships with other USDOT agencies and other transportation data providers and users inside and outside the federal government.

BTS began operations in late 1992; the Panel on Statistical Programs and Practices of the Bureau of Transportation Statistics began its study in January 1996. Drawing on panel members' experience in managing federal statistical agencies and other input, the panel reviewed BTS's current operations and considered its future goals in light of the characteristics and functions of an effective statistical agency and transportation data needs for policy planning and research.

THE NEED FOR IMPROVED TRANSPORTATION STATISTICS

Historically, the collection of data about transportation has been widely dispersed among numerous public and private agencies, each using its own standards and focused on a particular transportation mode (highways, airlines, railroads, etc.). The result is that considerable data are available about various aspects of transportation, but often the data are not comparable and not designed to inform policy issues that require a cross-modal, system-wide perspective. Previous studies (e.g., National Research Council, 1992a) have documented such problems as the lack of basic data on freight and passenger flows across transportation modes and the lack of comparable data across modes with which to evaluate such key aspects of the transportation system as safety, access, efficiency, and quality of service.

To bring a greater degree of coordination, comparability, and quality standards to transportation data and to fill important data gaps, the 1991 ISTEA established BTS and charged it with producing a *Transportation Statistics Annual Report*, developing intermodal data on commodity and passenger flows, and carrying out six functions:

(1) "compiling, analyzing, and publishing a comprehensive set of transportation statistics";

(2) "establishing and implementing, in cooperation with the modal administrators, the States, and other Federal officials, a comprehensive, long-term program for the collection and analysis of data relating to the performance of the national transportation system";

(3) "issuing guidelines for the collection of information by the Department of Transportation . . . to ensure that such information is accurate, reliable, relevant, and in a form that permits systematic analysis";

(4) "coordinating the collection of information by the Department of Transportation . . . with . . . other Federal departments and agencies and collecting appropriate data not elsewhere gathered";

(5) "making statistics . . . readily accessible"; and

(6) "identifying information that is needed . . . but which is not being collected . . . and making recommendations . . . concerning extramural and intramural research programs to provide such information."

The 1991 ISTEA explicitly established BTS as a *statistical* agency, not as a policy development office or an administrative unit. A statistical agency is expected not only to compile, analyze, and disseminate data for policy and public use, but also to work toward continued improvement of the relevance, timeliness, and quality of those data. In addition, a statistical agency provides leadership for its parent department in such areas as setting quality standards for data release and documentation, conducting evaluations and research on methods, developing key national indicators for policy use, and coordinating data collection in order to identify and fill gaps and reduce duplication and costs. A statistical agency is characterized by a strong measure of professional independence to ensure the objectivity and credibility of its data, high standards of quality and professionalism in all aspects of its work, and relationships of trust and openness with data providers and users (see National Research Council, 1992b).

ASSESSING BTS

During its short span of existence, BTS has accomplished a great deal. It has issued annual reports on the transportation system that have a strong analytical focus, produced compendia and guides to transportation data, sponsored major surveys on intermodal commodity flows and household travel, provided access to a wide range of transportation data on the World Wide Web and CD-ROMs, sponsored symposia and conferences, worked with other federal agencies to standardize geographic information systems, and initiated work with the Bureau of Economic Analysis to develop a fuller accounting of the transportation sector of the U.S. economy.

BTS could not expect to accomplish all of its assigned agenda at the outset, and it has not done so. As a strategic decision, BTS has focused primarily on compiling data and making them accessible (functions 1 and 5 in the ISTEA list) and deferred most work on the other functions enumerated in ISTEA. Also, although BTS has provided extensive amounts of data to users from a wide range of sources, it has not provided correspondingly detailed information to help users understand the quality and usefulness of alternative data sets. To date, BTS has functioned primarily as a data compilation and dissemination agency. It has yet to evolve into a statistical agency that fulfills a broad mandate to improve transportation data to address users' information needs.

The decision to concentrate on data compilation and dissemination has brought some advantages to BTS and its data users. BTS has demonstrated its capability to use the latest technologies for data delivery and to remain sensitive to its customers' expressed needs. In the panel's view, however, it is now critically important for BTS to take on the leadership functions assigned to it by the 1991 ISTEA to improve the relevance and quality of transportation data. To accomplish these goals, BTS must first develop a strong statistical staff and set an example of statistical excellence in its own operations.

REAUTHORIZATION

The case for a statistical agency within USDOT to develop transportation data for important policy purposes, particularly those that require a cross-modal, system-wide perspective, was made clear in earlier studies of transportation data needs and recognized in the 1991 ISTEA. BTS has made a good start on its mandate. It has begun to fill such important data gaps as passenger and freight movements, and it has brought together a large volume of transportation data in formats that are accessible to a wide range of users. It is the panel's view that BTS should be reauthorized to continue to perform these valuable information functions and to develop the other functions of a statistical agency.[1] Such an agency is required to coordinate and improve the decentralized database in the field of transportation.

*(1) We strongly recommend that the U.S. Congress reauthorize the Bureau of Transportation Statistics.

---

[1] Recommendations that pertain specifically to the reauthorization of BTS, as part of the reauthorization of ISTEA or such other legislative vehicle as the Congress deems appropriate, are starred (*). These are recommendations are 1, 3, 7, 9, and 10.

FOCUSING ON QUALITY

BTS to date has focused on making as much data as possible available to as broad a community of users as possible. BTS must now begin to focus on data quality, including comparability, accuracy (or bias), and variability. It should also focus on the relevance of transportation data in terms of appropriateness of concepts, the match between concepts, operational definitions, and measurements, the level of subject and geographic detail, and timeliness (see next section). BTS must help policy makers, planners, researchers, and other users distinguish useful, high-quality data from data that are suspect or inappropriate and identify priority areas for data improvement.

To ensure the quality of transportation data and provide statistical leadership for the department, BTS needs to increase the quantitative capabilities of its staff. While highly qualified in many ways, relatively few BTS staff have extensive training and experience in such areas as statistical sampling and survey design, advanced data collection and editing methods, index construction, statistical estimation on complex sample surveys, and related areas. BTS should focus immediate attention on strengthening the statistical and technical capabilities of its staff, particularly in determining qualifications and responsibilities for its authorized vacancies. It should also be authorized by the department to appoint an associate director at the Senior Executive Service level with extensive statistical knowledge and experience to direct methodological research, develop and oversee the implementation of data quality standards, and oversee programs for data evaluation and improvement. Finally, it should provide opportunities for continuing development of staff professional capabilities.

(2) BTS should be authorized to appoint an associate director for statistical methods and research at the Senior Executive Service level to provide leadership in improving the quality of transportation statistics. BTS should give priority to hiring highly qualified staff with expertise in statistical methods.

As a high priority, BTS should address its mandate in ISTEA to develop guidelines for data quality throughout USDOT. Indeed, the Congress should underscore the importance of focusing on the quality of transportation data by mandating that BTS develop written quality *standards,* working with the statistical units located in the other USDOT modal administrations, that will be binding throughout USDOT. BTS should also report periodically (every 2 years) on progress within USDOT to improve transportation data quality.

*(3) In the reauthorization of BTS, the Congress should strengthen current law by assigning responsibility to BTS to establish data quality standards, consistent with good statistical practice, that are binding throughout

USDOT and available for use by transportation agencies outside USDOT and for reference by the public. The reauthorization should also:
- **require the secretary of transportation to appoint a departmental standards committee, chaired by the BTS director and with representatives from the USDOT statistical units, to work with BTS in developing department-wide data quality standards and**
- **require BTS to prepare every 2 years a report to the Congress that identifies improvements achieved in data quality by BTS and the statistical units in the other USDOT modal administrations and in the provision of information about quality to data users.**

Another priority for BTS should be to improve the documentation of transportation data, not only to alert users to data errors and limitations, but also to provide the basis on which to develop in-depth evaluation and improvement programs for key data sets. BTS should develop comprehensive documentation for its own surveys, including user's guides and reports that describe methods and bring together information on sources and extent of errors. It should also identify improvements that can be made immediately in describing data from other sources that are included in its compendia, CD-ROMs, and World Wide Web site, while it works with the statistical units in the other USDOT modal administrations to develop more comprehensive documentation standards for the department.

(4) BTS should improve the documentation of the transportation data it makes available so that users can readily assess their quality, including accuracy, variability, and comparability across transportation modes and over time.

ENSURING RELEVANCE

To serve as a statistical agency for USDOT, BTS must address not only the quality, but also the relevance of transportation data for policy making, program planning, and research use. To this end, BTS should develop a broad vision of a comprehensive transportation data system that can serve the information needs of users over the long term, by asking key constituencies such questions as: What are important national policy concerns in transportation, how are they changing, and what are the implications for data? What changes are occurring in the economy and society that suggest needs for new data or reassignment of priorities among areas? What topics and information needs are still relevant from the past?

On the basis of its own vision and input from others, BTS should develop a structured implementation plan that specifies short-term, intermediate, and long-term activities and goals in each of its main programmatic areas. Such a plan is essential for BTS to cope with its large array of responsibilities and to make the most effective use of its resources.

(5) BTS should develop a long-term strategy for implementing fully all of the areas in its mandate in order to evolve as a statistical agency that ensures the relevance, as well as the quality, of transportation data. The implementation plan should set priorities within the context of a vision of a comprehensive system of transportation data.

The development of key national indicators—examples are monthly and quarterly estimates of gross domestic product, monthly unemployment rates, annual high school dropout rates—is an important means by which statistical agencies provide highly relevant data for the policy debate and general public awareness. Some indicators have direct effects on the economy and public- and private-sector decision making.

As it is mandated to do in the 1991 ISTEA, BTS should move quickly to become the focal point for the development of key national indicators on transportation that can serve policy makers and the general public. In working with other agencies inside and outside USDOT to develop appropriate indicators, BTS must pay careful attention to the concepts to be reflected in the new data series and take steps to ensure their accuracy, timeliness, and objectivity. Development of key indicators will also help BTS identify data sources that are needed for indicators that should receive priority attention for evaluation and improvement.

(6) BTS should develop key national statistical indicators for the transportation system—for example, multimodal series in the areas of safety, travel patterns, and the condition of the transportation infrastructure—in consultation with the statistical and analysis units in the other USDOT modal administrations and the transportation community.

Two other ways in which a statistical agency ensures data relevance are to coordinate data collection in its subject area to the extent feasible and to identify user needs. The 1991 ISTEA assigns BTS these responsibilities, which require interaction with other USDOT modal administrations and with public and private agencies outside USDOT.

As a means to facilitate the cost-effectiveness of data collection programs within USDOT, BTS should be authorized to compile a statistical budget for use by the secretary in making budget decisions. A compilation of the budget for all USDOT statistical activities and programs will help clarify what the individual modal administrations see as priorities and help the secretary determine how well those priorities accord with department-wide data needs.

Looking outside USDOT, state transportation agencies and metropolitan planning organizations (MPOs) play vital roles in transportation policy planning and investment and associated data collection and use and hence are important constituencies for BTS to learn from about user needs. BTS should develop regular channels of communication with states and MPOs, by building on the efforts it has already made to obtain input and feedback from them. BTS should also move forward with its plans to develop technical assistance programs for states and MPOs to help them apply transportation data—for example, the Commodity Flow Survey—for such purposes as economic development analysis and planning.

*(7) In the reauthorization of BTS, the Congress should require BTS to compile, analyze, and provide to the secretary of transportation a department-wide statistical program budget for the secretary's use in making decisions during the budget process.**

(8) BTS should regularly meet with representatives from states and metropolitan planning organizations to help determine priorities for key national statistical indicators, other data, analyses, products and services, and improvements in data concepts and measurements. BTS should also provide technical advice to states and metropolitan planning organizations to help them make more effective use of BTS and other transportation data.

BUILDING AN AGENCY

Statistical agencies must have a large measure of professional independence in order to ensure the credibility of the data they provide and to prevent any possibility of manipulation of statistics to serve particular political or policy purposes. The 1991 ISTEA includes several provisions that are intended to protect the independence of BTS; they should be extended and strengthened.

*(9) The reauthorization of BTS should continue the provisions of current law that the director of BTS be a presidential appointee with a fixed term of 4 years, who reports directly to the secretary of transportation and is a qualified professional with relevant training and experience. The reauthorization should underscore the professional independence of BTS by statutorily confirming its authority to release statistical information without prior clearance by political officials outside BTS.**

Statistical agencies must also have a relationship of trust with the respondents, both individuals and organizations, that provide them with data. Key to maintaining this relationship are procedures and practices that provide a firm guarantee of confidentiality of responses. The reauthorization of BTS should extend the provision in current law that BTS may not release data that could identify an individual or a business respondent.

Two programs that were recently transferred to BTS, the Office of Airline Information and the Motor Carrier Statistics Program, currently operate under regulations that provide for the release of data about individual businesses. BTS should review these programs to determine their compatibility with its mission as a statistical agency, which is to provide data for statistical purposes (not for program operation or regulation), and the advisability of transferring one or both programs elsewhere within USDOT.

*(10) **The reauthorization of BTS should continue to require that BTS not release data that could identify individual or business respondents.**

(11) **BTS should review the Office of Airline Information and Motor Carrier Statistics programs, which provide for the release of individually identifiable data, for their compatibility with the BTS mission as a statistical agency that is committed to confidentiality protection. To the extent that data from these programs need to be available in identifiable form to serve important policy purposes, BTS should recommend to the secretary that the programs be lodged elsewhere in USDOT.**

Finally, statistical agencies should exercise and be expected to exercise a leadership role in their departments in such areas as the development of data quality standards and coordination of data collection. In addition to providing BTS with greater statutory authority, as recommended earlier, BTS will need strong support from the department on a day-to-day basis to develop a leadership role. Over time, as BTS builds its staff capabilities (as recommended earlier) and gains a reputation for excellence in its own operations, it will be better able to work effectively with the other modal administrations in USDOT to improve the quality and relevance of transportation data for the department and the entire transportation community.

1

Introduction

The Bureau of Transportation Statistics (BTS) in the U.S. Department of Transportation (USDOT) is the newest agency in the federal statistical system. BTS was authorized by the Intermodal Surface Transportation Efficiency Act (ISTEA) of 1991 and began operations in late 1992. (A small staff group was assigned to work on setting up BTS in October 1992; the management order for BTS to begin operations was signed by the secretary in December 1992.) BTS's first director, T.R. Lakshmanan, was nominated a little more than a year later, in January 1994, and confirmed by the Senate in June 1994.

BTS joins a group of agencies—including the Bureau of the Census, the Bureau of Labor Statistics, the Energy Information Administration, the National Center for Education Statistics, and others—each of which has a mission to provide data and statistics in a broad subject area for public- and private-sector decision making, program planning and evaluation, research, and general public understanding. Although USDOT has from the beginning included statistical units with specialized responsibilities for data programs—such as the Safety Data Services Division in the Federal Aviation Administration, the Office of Highway Information Management in the Federal Highway Administration, the Office of Statistical and Economic Analysis in the Maritime Administration, and the National Center for Statistics and Analysis in the National Highway Traffic Safety Administration—BTS is the first statistical agency established in the department with a broad mandate.

The same ISTEA legislation that authorized BTS (see Appendix A) also called for a study of USDOT data collection procedures and capabilities by the National Academy of Sciences/National Research Council. The scope of the study was developed in the course of discussions with the Congress and USDOT, and in fall 1995 the Committee on National Statistics and the Transportation Research Board of the National Research Council established the Panel on Statistical Programs and Practices of the Bureau of Transportation Statistics.

The panel was charged to review the statistical programs of BTS and its practices to improve the quality and usefulness of transportation data throughout USDOT and the federal statistical system. It was asked to examine the functions that BTS does or could perform (e.g., statistical policy, data collection, analysis, dissemination) and its resources and capabilities to carry out those functions. The panel was asked to focus particularly on two areas: (1) the statistical policy functions of the agency vis-à-vis the department—such as coordinating data collection programs, providing standards for data collection and reporting, and providing guidance on confidentiality issues, documentation, and quality control and (2) the agency's relationships to other USDOT agencies, to other federal statistical agencies, and to other transportation data providers and users, such as state and metropolitan agencies.

In summary, the panel was asked to review BTS's functions, capabilities, resources, and relationships with other agencies. In developing and presenting its findings and recommendations, the panel illustrates its points with examples of transportation data needs, data collection programs, time-series indicators, and data quality assessments. However, the panel was neither charged nor constituted to carry out a review of transportation data programs or data needs as such, and it has not done so. For a comprehensive assessment of data requirements for national transportation policy making, see *Data for Decisions*, a report of a committee of the Transportation Research Board (National Research Council, 1992a). This report identified problems and gaps in needed data and indicators, particularly for analyses of policy issues that cut across transportation modes, and called for the establishment of a transportation data center—what ultimately became BTS.

METHODS OF STUDY

The collection and use of data for public purposes are prescribed by the U.S. Constitution (which requires a decennial census as the basis for apportionment of seats in the U.S. House of Representatives) and by many statutes. A number of federal statistical agencies can trace their history back 100 years or more. However, there is only a small literature that establishes criteria for effective statistical agencies (see, e.g., National Research Council, 1992b) or that examines what factors help them gain stature in their department, develop useful, high-quality, credible data series, and build strong ties with user communities.

This study of BTS therefore relies heavily on the experience and judgment of members of the panel who have directed other statistical agencies (or major programs in such agencies) or who have conducted reviews of the federal statistical system and individual agencies. (These members have contributed to the literature in this area—see, e.g., Bonnen, 1983, 1996; Groves, 1995; Mitroff, Mason, and Barabba, 1983; Norwood, 1995.) Because a statistical agency must operate within the context of its department and the set of user needs in its subject area, the panel relied on its members from the transportation community to assess the applicability of conclusions developed from observation of other federal statistical agencies to the situation facing BTS.

The panel obtained information on the operation of statistical programs in other parts of USDOT, learned about data needs of state departments of transportation and their assessment of BTS to date, reviewed BTS's budget and staffing plans and materials provided by BTS on its products and services and their users, and closely examined selected BTS products and services (including printed publications, CD-ROM data products, and the contents of BTS's World Wide Web site) on such dimensions as data quality and ease of use. The panel also looked at how other statistical agencies have implemented selected aspects of their operations, such as the development of data quality standards, relationships with state and local users and providers of data, and confidentiality protection for data provided by individual respondents. The recommendations developed by the panel reflect these inputs as they were evaluated by the panel members on the basis of their experience and judgment.

THE REPORT

The first part of Chapter 2 reviews the history and rationale that led to the establishment of BTS as a statistical agency with broad responsibilities in the area of transportation. Such an agency was late in coming to USDOT because of the historically strong orientation of transportation policy and associated data collection to particular transportation modes (highway, air, rail, etc.). However, the need for a statistical agency that continually works to coordinate and improve a wide range of transportation data programs to support cross-modal, system-wide policy planning and other purposes is clear. The second part of Chapter 2 compares BTS's accomplishments to date with its mandate from ISTEA and with the criteria for an effective statistical agency found in the literature and developed from panel members' experience and judgments. The panel's fundamental conclusion from this review is that BTS has made a good beginning in its very brief span of existence and should be reauthorized by the U.S. Congress.

The bulk of the report looks to the future. Chapter 3 discusses the priority that BTS should place on activities to improve the quality of transportation data. To date, while getting under way, BTS has focused primarily on data compilation and dissemination and less on data improvement. This orientation needs to change now. The chapter recommends provisions to include in the reauthorization of BTS to strengthen its role for data improvement in the department, as well as actions by BTS to develop the full range of statistical and analytical capabilities in its staff that are necessary to carry out its responsibilities.

Chapter 4 addresses BTS's program responsibilities to ensure the relevance of transportation data for policy making and other important user needs. These responsibilities include developing statistical series that can serve as indicators of key aspects of the transportation system and playing a stronger role in the coordination of transportation data collection inside and outside USDOT. The chapter also considers opportunities for BTS to assist key constituencies, including state transportation departments and metropolitan planning organizations, to make more effective use of BTS and other transportation data.

Finally, Chapter 5 considers institutional characteristics that are important for BTS to have. It recommends provisions that should be explicitly continued or added in the reauthorization of BTS to ensure that it continues as a statistical agency that is independent of policy or political control. To be successful over the long term, BTS must be able to function at the highest level of professional standards, objectivity, and credibility.

The appendices provide important background information or illustrate points made in the text through case studies. They include: references to BTS in the 1991 ISTEA (Appendix A); information about other statistical agencies inside and outside USDOT (Appendix B); a comparison of BTS with the principles and practices for a federal statistical agency expressed in a report of the Committee on National Statistics (National Research Council, 1992b) (Appendix C); a case study of improving airline safety statistics in BTS's annual statistical compendium, *National Transportation Statistics* (Appendix D); descriptions of selected CD-ROM products on the BTS World Wide Web site (Appendix E); and a case study of integrating data and filling data gaps for household travel surveys (Appendix F). The final appendix contains biographical sketches of panel members and staff (Appendix G).

A NOTE ON REAUTHORIZATION LEGISLATION

The Clinton administration has introduced a bill to reauthorize the 1991 ISTEA: the National Economic Crossroads Transportation Efficiency Act of 1997 (NEXTEA). The NEXTEA bill would reauthorize BTS for another 6 years, continue many of the provisions about BTS from the earlier legislation, and amend other provisions. We have developed recommendations about BTS independently, several of which call for changes to BTS's legislative authority. The rationale for these (and other) recommendations is developed in the body of the report. We hope that the Congress will give careful consideration to our recommendations when developing reauthorization legislation for BTS.

2

History and Assessment of BTS

TRANSPORTATION DATA PROGRAMS IN HISTORICAL PERSPECTIVE

Many of the major statistical agencies in cabinet departments—the Bureau of the Census, the Bureau of Labor Statistics, the National Agricultural Statistics Service, and others—were established decades ago (see Appendix B). However, no such agency existed in the U.S. Department of Transportation until the Bureau of Transportation Statistics (BTS) was authorized by the 1991 Intermodal Surface Transportation Efficiency Act (ISTEA), even though the federal government has funded transportation projects and been concerned with transportation issues for over 100 years. A primary reason is the long-standing orientation of transportation planning and investment—and the associated data collection and analysis—to specific modes of transportation (e.g., air, highway, mass transit, railroad, maritime) and not to the transportation system as a whole. The institutional structure for transportation planning and investment, in which states, localities, and the private sector play key roles, also helps explain the high degree of decentralization that has historically characterized transportation data development and use.

Modally Oriented, Decentralized Data Development

The Federal Role

The U.S. Department of Transportation (USDOT), established in 1967, is organized along modal lines (see Appendix B for information on the modal administrations and their statistical units). BTS is treated as a modal administration: it is a separate agency, whose director reports directly to the secretary of transportation. The BTS director is appointed by the president with the consent of the Senate for a term of 4 years.

Most of USDOT's modal administrations antedate the department. For example, an Office of Road Inquiry, the ultimate predecessor to the Federal Highway Administration, was established in 1893 in the U.S. Department of Agriculture: its functions included data collection and analysis related to highways. Federal funding of state highway projects was first legislated in 1916. The Air Commerce Act of 1926 established the predecessor of the Federal Aviation Administration in the U.S. Department of Commerce. Federal support for railroads dates back even further, to the Civil War. When USDOT was established as an entity in 1967, the Federal Highway Administration, the Federal Aviation Administration, and the other modal administrations that were brought under the departmental umbrella continued to a large extent to operate at arm's length from one another.

Similarly, the major data collection programs in USDOT largely developed within and for the various modal administrations. These programs include data on highway conditions; daily travel patterns of households; operating characteristics, freight and passenger miles and revenues, and accidents and fatalities for highways, airlines, railroads, etc.; and many other topics. Some of these programs obtain data through cooperative efforts with state agencies and local officials; other programs obtain data from sample surveys of households and businesses; and still other programs obtain data as a by-product of reports of transportation providers (e.g., airlines, railroads, trucking firms) for regulatory and monitoring purposes.

During the first decade of USDOT's existence (roughly 1967-1977), the department had a strong planning orientation, and the Office of the Secretary invested in cross-cutting, intermodal data systems to complement and strengthen the programs in the modal administrations. It helped fund Bureau of the Census surveys every 5 years of freight or commodity flows (as part of the economic census program) and of long-distance household travel. Regulatory activities of such agencies as the Interstate Commerce Commission and the Civil Aeronautics Board also generated substantial amounts of data, although they were largely specific to a transportation mode.

Subsequently, key sources of data were lost or allowed to lapse. Deregulation of airlines, railroads, bus companies, and trucking companies resulted in reductions in the data collected. Between 1977 and 1992, when BTS began operations, USDOT did not sponsor intermodal commodity or household travel flow surveys.

States, Localities, and the Private Sector

The institutional structure for transportation in the United States involves large investment and operational responsibilities by agencies outside the federal government. States and local governments account for the largest share of all government expenditures on transportation. (In 1992, total government expenditures for transportation infrastructure investments, operating subsidies, and other expenses amounted to $113 billion, of which state and local governments accounted for 69 percent from their own revenues and another 19 percent from federal grants.) Private investment in transportation equipment and structures is also significant—$95 billion in 1992, primarily for equipment. (Total public and private expenditures, including investment and operations, attributed to transportation-related final demand in estimates of the U.S. gross domestic product amounted to $642 billion in 1992 and $725 billion in 1994.)[1]

As noted earlier, some of the data collection programs in USDOT rely on cooperative arrangements with state and local agencies. Such agencies have historically collected large amounts of data for their own use, as well as to support federal needs, which provide important information on the performance and condition of the transportation system.

State highway departments (now state departments of transportation, DOTs) were some of the first agencies to collect data on travel patterns in the United States during the 1920s. Today, state DOTs collect data on bridge and road conditions, congestion levels, multimodal passenger ridership, freight movement, vehicle use characteristics, vehicle fleet mix, and accidents, as well as supplementary data that relate to the impacts of transportation investment (e.g., tourism expenditures, construction dollars, jobs created). At the metropolitan and local level, metropolitan planning organizations (MPOs) and local transportation agencies collect large amounts of data that provide the basis for decisions on regional and local investments. Local providers of transportation services, such as transit agencies, collect data on ridership volumes and customer characteristics.

Regional and local transportation agencies and transportation researchers have for decades spent substantial time and resources to understand travel behavior patterns and the socioeconomic determinants of such travel. They have a long history of using travel surveys, census data, and market research in the development and use of travel forecasting methods.

Outside the public sector, users of the transportation system collect and use data for their own decision-making purposes. Trucking and rail companies, for example, collect large amounts of data on freight shipments, travel times and delays, and commodity flows. Although such data would be useful as part of the infrastructure planning process, their proprietary nature often precludes such use. Associations of transportation users, such as trucking and railroad trade associations, have long-established systems for collecting data that are shared among members and accessible to others.

---

[1] Source for estimates: Bureau of Transportation Statistics (1996b:Tables 2-1, 2-11).

Conclusions

This brief historical review suggests several critical characteristics of the institutional environment for transportation data collection and analysis that have implications for the new BTS:

(1) The governmental structure for transportation investment in the United States is based on principles of federalism. States provide a basic foundation for many of the decisions that are made on such investment.

(2) Metropolitan planning and local transportation agencies have been actively involved in transportation investment decision making for many years.

(3) Consequently, state, metropolitan, and local agencies have been collecting transportation data for a long time. When combined with the data collection activities of private companies, the constituency for both quality data collection efforts and the effective use of these data is immense.

(4) USDOT has collected data, especially on the nation's highway system by working with the states, for many years. There are significant data collection and analysis capabilities located in several modal administrations of USDOT.

(5) Existing transportation data systems, whether developed by USDOT, state, metropolitan, or local agencies, or the private sector, are largely specific to particular transportation modes or specific regions or other areas. Comparable data for analysis of transportation issues across modes on a nationwide basis have largely been lacking.

The Need for Broad-Based Transportation Data

A strategic planning initiative by USDOT in the late 1980s led the Office of the Secretary and others inside and outside the department to realize that there were major gaps and deficiencies in available transportation data for policy purposes. Although recognizing that the large number of public and private transportation data sets served many important purposes, the Office of the Secretary found that most of the available data did not readily support cross-modal, system-wide analysis. Definitions and quality standards varied, and there were no up-to-date nationwide data on household travel and the shipment of goods across modes.

The department's Statement of National Transportation Policy (U.S. Department of Transportation, 1990:112) concluded:

> Gaps in transportation data include statistics on domestic and international flows of freight and passenger traffic by all modes, the extent and performance of intermodal connections, the financial and operating characteristics of smaller carriers, and the costs of both for-hire and private transportation incurred by each sector of the economy. While periodic evaluations of the extent, conditions, and performance of transportation facilities, equipment, and services are reported for some modes, they are very limited for others. Multimodal assessments of the entire transportation system to support strategic planning have not been regularly produced in a decade.

The statement committed USDOT to "develop a comprehensive assessment of data needs and priorities of the Department and the transportation community" and to "develop more effective and permanent institutional mechanisms" to improve transportation data coverage, quality, and availability, including linkages among the data collected by different agencies.

Shortly thereafter, a committee of the NRC Transportation Research Board (TRB) reviewed information needs for national transportation policy making. The committee concluded in its report, *Data for Decisions* (National Research Council, 1992a:45), that "substantial data exist about the transportation system, but fall short of providing the information needed to inform policy makers about the strategic issues facing the U.S. Department of Transportation."

Interestingly, the TRB committee distinguished between *data*, the direct product of a collection process, and *information*, which is data that are processed, organized, interpreted, and communicated to be useful in the context of specific decisions or problems (see Bonnen, 1977). The TRB committee determined that, although many types of data were available in the transportation area, these data often did not represent useful information for addressing transportation policy issues. Two specific deficiencies that the TRB committee and others identified were:

- the lack of data on freight and passenger flows across modes, which means that there was no basis with which to develop information on patterns and trends in the movement of people and goods locally, regionally, nationally, or cross-nationally, and
- the lack of comparability across modes of data in many key areas of performance, including: safety; access to services by such groups as elderly, disabled, low-income, and rural populations; and the efficiency and quality of service provided by the transportation system. Such lack of comparability precluded using the available data for such purposes as determining trouble spots in the system and conducting cost-benefit analyses of alternative transportation investments.

The TRB committee recommended that a transportation data center be established within USDOT. The center should: develop a national transportation performance monitoring system; issue a biennial report about the state of transportation; take responsibility for national passenger and freight flow surveys; engage in cooperative activities with other transportation data providers, including other USDOT modal administrations, to develop links among existing data sources and identify data gaps; and establish mechanisms for obtaining user input on transportation data needs. The transportation data center was envisioned as building bridges to other data programs rather than supplanting them.

With regard to organizational placement, the TRB committee observed (National Research Council, 1992a:9) that:

Many federal agencies have developed and sustained broad data programs to support agency mission objectives by establishing central statistical offices, such as the National Center for Education Statistics . . . . Organization of [the transportation data center] should be modeled on the best elements of other statistical agencies . . . [which] function as separate offices with permanent staff and separate budgets, command a strong measure of independence within their agencies to ensure the impartiality and credibility of the data they produce, and have a commitment to quality and professional standards.

The TRB committee sent a letter to Congress while it was considering the ISTEA legislation during 1991, laying out the committee's concerns about data and the options for recommendations that it was considering. (The committee's full report was published subsequent to passage of the ISTEA.) At about the same time, a panel of the National Academy of Public Administration (NAPA) reached a similar conclusion about the desirability of establishing a statistical agency with a broad mandate within USDOT. In August 1991, the NAPA panel stated that "a strong organizational focus is needed in the Department to develop adequate transportation statistics on a continuing basis" (National Academy of Public Administration, 1991).

ISTEA

The 1991 ISTEA (see Appendix A for relevant excerpts) provided for a Bureau of Transportation Statistics. The legislation charged BTS with producing a *Transportation Statistics Annual Report (TSAR)* and with carrying out the following six functions:

(1) "compiling, analyzing, and publishing a comprehensive set of transportation statistics," covering a range of topics (see Appendix A);

(2) "establishing and implementing, in cooperation with the modal administrators, the States, and other Federal officials, a comprehensive, long-term program for the collection and analysis of data relating to the performance of the national transportation system";

(3) "issuing guidelines for the collection of information by the Department of Transportation . . . to ensure that such information is accurate, reliable, relevant, and in a form that permits systematic analysis";

(4) "coordinating the collection of information by the Department of Transportation . . . with . . . other Federal departments and agencies and collecting appropriate data not elsewhere gathered";

(5) "making statistics . . . readily accessible"; and

(6) "identifying information that is needed . . . but which is not being collected . . . and making recommendations . . . concerning extramural and intramural research programs to provide such information."

In another section, the ISTEA established the Office of Intermodalism in the Office of the Secretary and required that office, among other functions, to work through BTS to develop, maintain, and disseminate intermodal transportation data, including data on commodity and passenger flows. Finally, the legislation stated that nothing in it should be construed to authorize BTS to require any other department or agency to collect data or to reduce the authority of any other officer of USDOT to collect and disseminate data independently. In other words, BTS was to take direct responsibility for intermodal data and provide leadership to identify information needs but work cooperatively with the modal administrations to obtain relevant data from their collection programs and other sources.

Why a Statistical Agency

Congress could have chosen some organizational structure other than a separate statistical agency by which to remedy the gaps and deficiencies in transportation data. For example, it could have attached data improvement responsibilities to a policy analysis or research office in the Office of the Secretary. (The department's efforts early in its existence to obtain system-wide data were carried out through the Office of the Secretary.) Alternatively, it could have set up an administrative unit oriented primarily to *data compilation and dissemination* functions—that is, to pulling together and distributing data as broadly as possible, perhaps also including cross-modal analyses of the data. Instead, the 1991 ISTEA called for a *statistical* agency, to which it assigned, in addition to data compilation, analysis, and dissemination, such functions as the establishment and maintenance of statistical standards, the development of national indicators for policy use, coordination of data collection programs, and long-range planning to identify and fill unmet user needs for information. In other words, the ISTEA called for a statistical agency that would perform all the activities necessary to turn data into high-quality, relevant statistical series and other useful information for policy-making, planning, and research purposes.

A report of the Committee on National Statistics (CNSTAT), *Principles and Practices for a Federal Statistical Agency* (National Research Council, 1992b:4-7), identifies key characteristics of an effective statistical agency. (Appendix C compares the current structure and operations of BTS with the criteria in the CNSTAT report.) An effective statistical agency must:

- be established as a separate entity with a strong and clearly defined mission that includes responsibility for assessing needs for information and determining sources of data, measurement methods, and efficient methods of collecting and ensuring the public availability of needed data;
- have a strong measure of independence in order to ensure credibility and objectivity and protect against the actuality or appearance of political manipulation of data;

- adhere to high standards of quality and professionalism in all aspects of its work;
- disseminate data and information about data quality widely and openly;
- maintain credibility with data providers, especially by having effective procedures to protect the confidentiality of individual responses to surveys and other data collection programs;
- seek input and advice on its programs and operations from data users and professional and technical experts;
- have an active research program in relevant substantive and methodological areas that supports user needs for information and improvements in statistical series while remaining policy-neutral; and
- coordinate with other agencies to promote data linkages and increase the productivity of the federal statistical system overall.

A statistical agency does not necessarily or even typically have responsibility for all of the data collection programs in a department. For example, a program office may sponsor surveys for program evaluation purposes, or an administrative unit may collect and disseminate data in a specialized area, particularly when those data are developed from an administrative records system. However, a statistical agency generally manages the major, general-purpose data collection programs of a department. Also, it provides advice to other parts of the department on data collection and analysis and should serve as statistical adviser to the secretary. Moreover, it provides leadership for the department in such areas as setting quality standards for data release and documentation and conducting methodological research on sample design, questionnaire development, evaluation of estimates, and other aspects of data collection and analysis programs.

The CNSTAT report states that the functions of a statistical agency do not belong in a policy analysis shop. A statistical agency should provide data that are policy-relevant and should engage in analysis that interprets the meaning and identifies the limitations of data for policy and other purposes. However, it must remain neutral with regard to policy options in order to maintain credibility.

On the issue of setting up a data compilation and dissemination unit as opposed to a statistical agency, the CNSTAT report (National Research Council, 1992b:10) states:

> One reason for establishing a separate statistical agency, rather than leaving statistical data compilation and dissemination activities as a part of a larger administrative operation, is to emphasize the principles and qualities of an effective statistical agency, for example, professional standards and confidentiality, as well as consistency of classifications or breadth of coverage. Another reason is to encourage research and the development of new information in a particular area of public interest.

The reviews of transportation data needs conducted to date, which include the TRB committee review (National Research Council, 1992a) and a section on

"The State of the Statistics" in the first *Transportation Statistics Annual Report* (Bureau of Transportation Statistics, 1994b:177-199), support these motives for establishing a statistical agency with a broad mandate within USDOT. Recurring themes are the lack of comparability across data sets and the lack of data systems to support cross-modal, system-wide analysis—in other words, the lack of useful information for transportation policy analysis, program planning, and research. Many of the specific priorities identified require coordination among agencies inside and outside USDOT and sustained work to improve data comparability and quality and to develop conceptual frameworks for key statistics.

As just one example, a TRB review of data needs for truck safety in the late 1980s found significant discrepancies in estimates of the number of nonfatal truck crashes reported by the National Highway Traffic Safety Administration, the Federal Highway Administration, and the private National Safety Council, due largely to differences in the definitions of "crash" and "truck." The review also found significant variation in estimates of the rates of fatal and nonfatal truck accidents per mile of travel because of the lack of detailed data on truck travel that were consistent over a period of years to serve as the denominators for accident rates (National Research Council, 1990:12-13). Since publication of that review, improvements have been made in truck safety data, although more remains to be done.

The TRB committee report, *Data for Decisions* (National Research Council, 1992a:91), concluded that "the ad hoc, incremental approaches of the past have not been successful in creating a sustained consistent base of information, which is necessary to the secretary's national policy, advisory, and decision-making functions." Both the TRB committee and the NAPA advisory panel stressed the importance of having a strong agency within the department that could provide continuity and a long-term perspective for improving transportation data for policy planning and other purposes. The case for a statistical agency within USDOT with a broad mandate was made clear.

ASSESSING BTS

Experience with the development of national statistics suggests that it takes many years to develop the capabilities, stature, and credibility required for an effective statistical agency in a cabinet department (see, e.g., Duncan and Shelton, 1978; Norwood, 1995). BTS is very young—only 4 years old; it could not be expected to accomplish all of its mandate from the 1991 ISTEA nor to meet all of the criteria for an effective statistical agency in such a short time, and it has not done so. We review BTS's start-up operations and achievements during the first authorization period—they are considerable although concentrated on particular aspects of its mandate. We also indicate areas and functions that, to date, BTS has addressed to only a limited extent but that must be developed for it to evolve into an effective statistical agency for USDOT.

The Start-Up Years

A major achievement of BTS has been getting the agency organized and staffed. Beginning with a staff of 4 people in October 1992, the agency grew to 37 people by fall 1996, of which 16 were in the Office of Airline Information (OAI). (The OAI was originally part of the Civil Aeronautics Board. It was transferred to the Office of the Secretary in 1984 when the Civil Aeronautics Board went out of business, transferred again to the Research and Special Programs Administration, and then transferred to BTS in May 1995.) BTS is authorized to have 60 full-time-equivalent staff through 1997, of which 20 positions are for OAI. BTS has made progress in filling its vacancies but still has a significant number of authorized vacant positions.

From the beginning, the BTS staff have exhibited high levels of energy and enthusiasm. They are clearly excited to be building a new agency from the ground up and have worked hard to develop and provide products and services to the transportation community. They have made an impressive start in developing BTS output, which includes programs and services that we describe below, organized in terms of the specific mandates for BTS in the 1991 ISTEA (see Appendix A).

Annual Reports

BTS has to date produced three of the *Transportation Statistics Annual Reports (TSARs)* that are mandated in section 6006.f of the 1991 ISTEA (Bureau of Transportation Statistics, 1994b). The first was produced within 15 months of the agency's operational start and provided an overview of the entire system. Subsequent reports have updated that overview and in addition have emphasized particular themes—for example, productivity of the transportation sector in the 1995 report and environmental effects of transportation in the 1996 report.

Intermodal Data on Commodity and Passenger Flows

In response to section 5002.c.4 of the 1991 ISTEA, BTS assumed responsibility for planning and contracting with the Census Bureau for the conduct of the 1993 Commodity Flow Survey and the 1995 American Travel Survey. These are the first surveys in over 15 years to provide data on how freight and people move around in the United States, taking account of all modes of transportation. Summary reports for all 50 states and a national report from the Commodity Flow Survey have been released; more detailed electronic products are planned. The first reports from the American Travel Survey are scheduled for release in summer 1997. BTS has also contributed funds for related surveys sponsored by other USDOT modal administrations, such as the Nationwide Personal Transportation Survey sponsored by the Office of Highway Information Management in the Federal Highway Administration. (The Nationwide Personal Transportation Survey provides data primarily on daily, short-trip household travel, whereas the American Travel Survey provides data on longer trips.)

Broad Functional Areas Mandated by the ISTEA

Functions 1 and 5 During its start-up period, BTS emphasized two related functions of the six broad areas assigned to it by section 6006.c of the 1991 ISTEA: function 1: compiling, analyzing, and publishing a comprehensive set of transportation data; and function 5: making such data readily accessible. BTS has used both printed and computerized media for compilation and dissemination purposes. In contrast to the practice of most statistical agencies, BTS's data products have so far been provided at no charge to users (with the exception that OAI, following its long-standing practice, charges fees for its products that are set to recover the costs of distribution).

Published products include the annual *TSARs*, which include an analysis for each year of transportation data in a particular area of policy interest. In addition, BTS has produced compendia and guides that bring together many data series and describe the range of public and private transportation data sources and how to find out about them (see Table 2-1). BTS has just begun a peer-reviewed semiannual *Journal of Transportation and Statistics*, which will provide an outlet for studies and analyses that feature aspects of transportation data use and methods. The plan for the *Journal* is for papers to be contributed by staff and solicited from academic researchers and other data users in the field.

Detailed analysis of data requires access to computer-readable data products, and BTS has made numerous transportation data sets available on CD-ROMs and data diskettes. Its first CD-ROM was the Transportation Data Sampler-1, containing selected databases and reports from USDOT modal administrations and other sources. This product was produced in time to be provided to the thousands of people who attended the January 1993 annual meeting of the Transportation Research Board, just a month after the BTS staff first thought of the idea and only a few months after BTS began operations.

BTS has also looked to computer technology to facilitate communication among people working in the transportation field. One of its CD-ROM products is the State and Metropolitan Analysis for Regional Transportation (SMART) CD-ROM, which contains such reference documents as video clips, guidance materials, case studies, dissertations, and surveys, as well as data sets submitted to BTS by MPOs and state DOTs. The purpose of the SMART project is to assist MPO and state DOT planners in responding to the increased planning requirements of the ISTEA and the 1990 Clean Air Act Amendments.

Furthermore, BTS has devoted considerable time and resources to developing and maintaining its home page on the Internet World Wide Web (see Figure 2-1). The ambitious goal of the BTS web site is to serve as a means by which

TABLE 2-1 Printed Periodic Publications of the Bureau of Transportation Statistics

Publication	Frequency	Comments
Directory of Transportation Data Sources	Annual beginning December 1993	Provides one-page abstracts for each data source listed; 1993 volume totaled 330 pages, including entries for USDOT, other federal agency, and United Nations data sources; 1996 volume totaled 649 pages, including entries for USDOT, other federal agency, United Nations, state, private organization, Canadian, and Mexican data sources
Journal of Transportation and Statistics	Twice yearly, beginning 1997	To contain peer-reviewed articles that feature aspects of transportation data use and methodology
National Transportation Statistics (NTS)	Annual beginning 1993 under BTS (published previously by the Research and Special Programs Administration)	Compendium of statistical series for all modes of transportation on performance, safety, costs, energy use, and other topics, compiled from USDOT and other sources; 1993 volume contained 98 tables and 52 charts, with data back to 1960 when possible; 1996 volume contained 134 tables and 42 charts

Transportation Expressions	Two editions to date (1994, 1996)	Comprehensive inventory of transportation terms and definitions with references to specific source; examples of terms include Available Seat Mile (2 definitions), Fatality (5 definitions), Mode (4 definitions), Semitrailer (2 definitions)
Transportation Statistics Annual Report (TSAR)	Annual beginning 1994	Analyzes the state of transportation and transportation statistics; 1994 volume provided overviews of use of the system, performance, costs, safety, energy, and the environment; 1995 volume included special section on the economic performance of transportation; 1996 volume included special section on transportation and the environment; 1997 volume will feature transportation access and mobility
Transportation Statistics Forum	To be determined, to begin in 1997	Newsletter to serve as a two-way channel of communication between BTS and transportation data users

SOURCE: Panel on Statistical Programs and Practices of the Bureau of Transportation Statistics, National Research Council, 1997.

NOTE: Excludes topical and special reports not regularly published.

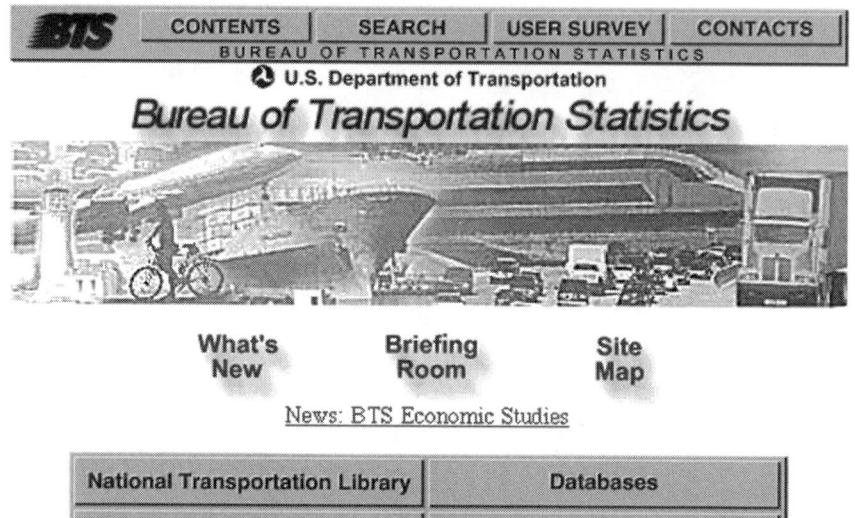

FIGURE 2-1 BTS home page on the World Wide Web (www.bts.gov).

planners and researchers in all levels of government as well as in the private sector can learn of the full range of available data and analyses that pertain to transportation. In addition, the site is meant to serve as a vehicle to put transportation analysts and planners in touch with one another to share knowledge and information.

The site provides direct access to selected reports and data outputs (e.g., tables of trade flows between the United States and Mexico), together with descriptions of other data sources and links to the home pages of other USDOT modal administrations from which data can be obtained. In addition, the site includes the National Transportation Library, which provides under more than a dozen headings the full text of transportation-related reports, analyses, and papers obtained from private and public sources (see Figure 2-2). The emphasis in developing the site has been on making as many links as possible to sources of data. To date, BTS has paid relatively little attention to the quality or completeness of the documentation that needs to accompany the data for their effective use.

Functions 2, 3, 4, 6   The other four broad functions that are assigned to BTS in section 6006.c of the 1991 ISTEA are: (2) developing a data collection and analysis program in cooperation with the modal administrators, states, and other federal officials for monitoring the national transportation system; (3) issuing guidelines for data collection in USDOT to ensure that the resulting information is accurate, reliable, relevant, and usable; (4) coordinating data collection by

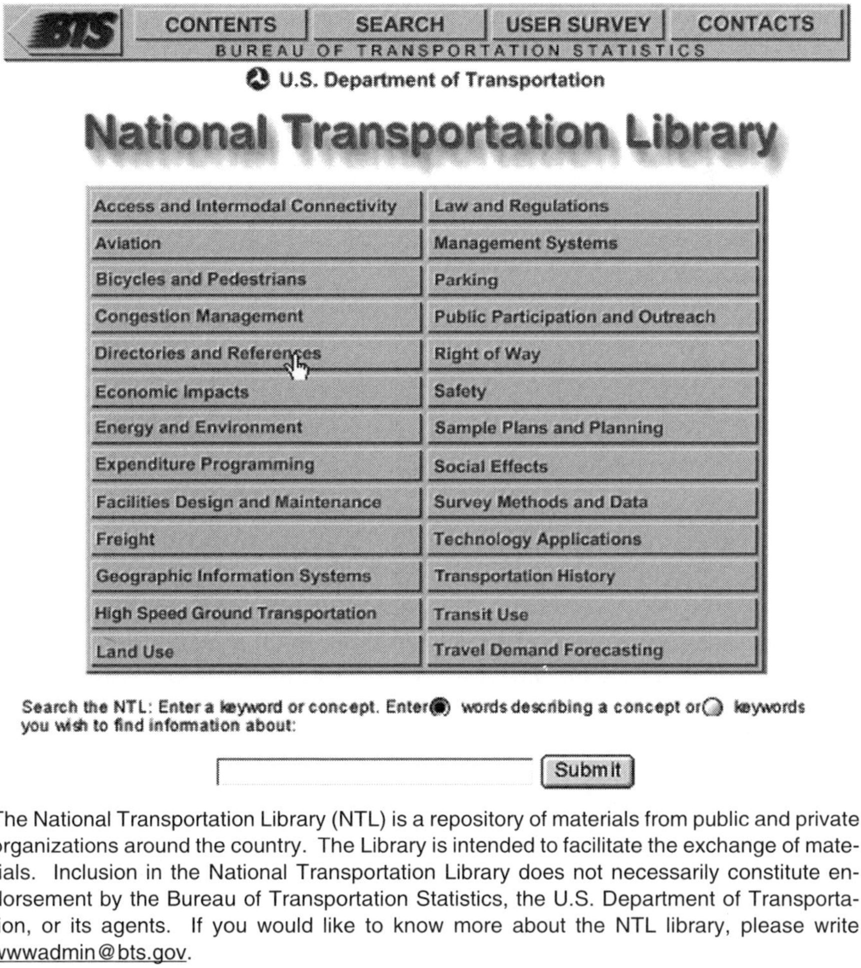

FIGURE 2-2   National Transportation Library page from the BTS web site.

USDOT with related activities of other federal agencies and collecting data to fill gaps; and (6) identifying unmet information needs and recommending research programs to provide such information. These areas are more difficult to address, and to date BTS has devoted relatively little effort to them, although it has taken first steps in some of them.

Specific activities that BTS has undertaken with other USDOT modal administrations, other federal agencies, and states and localities in the areas of data development, standards, and identification of unmet needs for information include the following:

- At the request of the modal administrations, BTS provides assistance in preparing materials required for clearance of their surveys by the U.S. Office of Management and Budget.
- Working with and on behalf of the entire transportation community, BTS analyzed the implications of possible changes in the year 2000 decennial census that could jeopardize the availability of small-area data on commuting patterns, and it is continuing to monitor the situation (Bureau of Transportation Statistics, 1996a).
- BTS is active in an interagency committee—the Federal Geographic Data Committee (FGDC)—that is developing standards for geographic information systems (GIS) for mapping and analyzing geospatial data.
- BTS provides funding for six standing committees of the Transportation Research Board, which obtain and distribute papers from transportation researchers and other users on information needs and data applications in several areas (freight transportation data; geographic information systems for transportation; travel survey methods; and national, statewide, and urban transportation data and information systems).
- BTS negotiated a memorandum of understanding with the Bureau of Economic Analysis in the U.S. Department of Commerce by which BEA will work with BTS staff in developing a transportation satellite account. When linked to the National Income and Product Accounts, the transportation satellite account should provide a more complete picture of the role of transportation in the economy (Bureau of Economic Analysis-Bureau of Transportation Statistics Working Group, 1996).
- BTS is developing ways to work more closely with state DOTs and MPOs to identify their information needs; to consider the appropriate role of federal, state, and local agencies in data collection and dissemination; to review the implications of technological advances for data collection and dissemination; and to develop means of technical assistance to states and localities to make more effective use of national transportation data sets. To date, BTS has conducted interviews with officials in selected states and sponsored a conference in spring 1997 for state and local officials jointly with the Federal Highway Administration, the Federal Transit Administration, the American Association of State Highway and

Transportation Officials, and the Association of Metropolitan Planning Organizations. (The Conference on Information Needs to Support State and Local Transportation Decisionmaking into the 21st Century was organized by the Transportation Research Board.)

• BTS has made a priority for fiscal 1998 to begin work with the other modal administrations to develop relevant and timely indicators of the national transportation system.

Discussion

Despite the initial efforts described above to carry out the full mandate of the ISTEA, the primary focus of BTS's efforts to date has been on functions 1 and 5—bringing together and making available a wide range of transportation data, references, and analytical materials in formats that are readily accessible by users. In other words, BTS has operated primarily as a data compilation and dissemination agency. It has not yet evolved into a statistical agency that fulfills a broad mandate to improve the quality and relevance of transportation data to address users' information needs.

The initial strategy to concentrate on data compilation and dissemination—a deliberate choice by the agency at the outset—has had some advantages for the transportation community and for BTS. First, it has helped BTS cope as a tiny, brand-new agency inserted into a department with a number of powerful and long-established entities. BTS has started two important intermodal surveys; for existing data programs from the other modal administrations and other sources, it has described these programs, acted as a conduit for information from them, and made them better known. In this way, BTS has positioned itself to build relationships with the other modal administrations and with other providers of data. Second, BTS's efforts to compile and disseminate a broad range of transportation data have made it easier for users to locate and obtain relevant numbers and data sets. In fact, BTS is far along in providing needed "one-stop shopping" services for transportation data users who otherwise must cope with a highly decentralized set of public and private data-producing organizations. Finally, an emphasis on data compilation and dissemination, particularly through high-technology means, has made BTS more visible to the user community. In effect, this emphasis has helped BTS "get on the map."

Statistics on the use of BTS's products and services suggest steady growth in the number of transportation analysts and other users who are obtaining data products and other forms of assistance from BTS. For example, calls to the BTS hotline for technical assistance increased from 10 per month in 1993 to 244 per month in 1996, and orders of BTS data products (publications, CD-ROMs, diskettes) increased from 750 per month in the last half of 1994 (when BTS began to build a customer database) to 4,455 per month in 1996. (BTS customer data indicate that, over the 2.5-year period, 55 percent of individual customers have placed repeat orders: the median number of products ordered by repeat customers is 4.)

Increases in orders, telephone calls for assistance, hits on the BTS web site, and similar statistics, however, require careful interpretation. They do not indicate, except very indirectly, the extent to which BTS customers find its data products and services useful. A customer satisfaction survey that BTS expects to mail to 6,000 customers in summer 1997 and other smaller-scale surveys of BTS users will provide some information on this point. However, such surveys are not likely to indicate the extent to which BTS products and services are helping users to gain improved understanding of transportation policy issues and behavior, nor the extent to which they are providing effective support for public- and private-sector decision making—the ultimate purposes of statistical information programs. Such outcomes are likely to become apparent only over time.

Discussions with representatives of other USDOT modal administrations and with such key constituencies as state officials provide subjective evidence that BTS has become visible to the user community and is believed to be making a positive contribution. These users value BTS's role in bringing together disparate data sets and providing convenient access to a wide range of data sources and reports that bear on transportation issues. They perceive BTS as an objective, honest provider of transportation data and data services.

RECOMMENDATION

Reviews that others have conducted of the modal orientation of transportation data programs and the consequent lack of comparable cross-modal and intermodal information to support policy planning and other purposes underline the need for a statistical agency for USDOT with a broad mandate. Our review of the activities and performance of BTS to date lead us to conclude that BTS has made a strong start in beginning to fulfill its mandate from the 1991 ISTEA. We therefore unequivocally endorse the reauthorization of BTS as part of the reauthorization of the ISTEA or in such other legislative vehicle as the Congress deems appropriate.

Reauthorization of BTS is necessary to ensure that the agency is able to continue to provide useful data compilation, analysis, and dissemination services. Also, reauthorization is necessary so that BTS can further develop the expertise and technical capabilities for an effective statistical agency and carry out all of the activities that are required to enhance the quality and relevance of transportation data and turn them into useful information for the department and transportation community at large.

(1) We strongly recommend that the U.S. Congress reauthorize the Bureau of Transportation Statistics.

3

Focusing on Data Quality

A statistical agency must be more than a data compilation and dissemination agency. It must create useful information, which means that it must focus on documenting, evaluating, and improving the quality and relevance of the data within its subject area. Without such a focus, resources are likely to be wasted—both by the statistical agency in compiling and disseminating data that are of poor quality or not relevant to analysis needs and by policy makers, planners, and researchers who are left to work with deficient or inappropriate data. To ensure data quality and relevance for its users while working to minimize costs and burden on data providers, a statistical agency must also keep pace with advances in data collection and statistical and analytical methods and techniques.

The Bureau of Transportation Statistics (BTS) should begin now to devote more of its attention to data documentation, evaluation, and improvement, even if it means slowing down its efforts to be a one-stop-shopping source for users of every available transportation data set. Many state transportation officials and other users from whom we heard are looking to BTS to help them sort through the mass of available information to distinguish those data that are better and more appropriate for their needs from data that are of lesser quality and usefulness. BTS needs not only to help users in this regard, but also to work to improve the available base of information for addressing important transportation policy issues and research questions. The 1991 Intermodal Surface Transportation Efficiency Act (ISTEA) recognized the need for a statistical agency with a broad mandate to provide leadership for transportation data improvement by stipulating that BTS issue guidelines to ensure that the information from the U.S. Department of Transportation (USDOT) is accurate, reliable, relevant, and in a form that permits systematic analysis.

"Quality" and "relevance" are multidimensional attributes of data, each of which requires attention by a statistical agency.[1] In this chapter, we define what we mean by "quality," which encompasses the comparability, accuracy, and variability of the data from a measurement system. BTS needs to focus immediately on data quality to qualify its initial emphasis on making as many kinds of data as widely available as possible. To make such a focus possible, BTS needs to strengthen the statistical and technical capabilities of its staff. The remainder of this chapter first discusses staffing requirements for BTS and then considers priority activities for BTS in the data quality area. Such activities include the development of quality standards for USDOT and improvements in the documentation of available data, both to assist data users and to provide the basis for continuing evaluation and improvement of transportation data systems. The committee's primary recommendations appear at the end of the chapter.

In Chapter 4, we define what we mean by "relevance," which encompasses the appropriateness of concepts, definitions, and measurements, the level of subject and geographic detail, and the timeliness of data from a measurement system. Chapter 4 discusses activities, some of immediate priority and others that represent longer-term goals, for BTS to ensure the relevance of transportation data for policy making and other purposes.

DIMENSIONS OF QUALITY

"Data quality" concerns the effects of how measurement systems are designed and conducted.[2] Dimensions of data quality include:

• *Comparability across data systems and time* (e.g., for cross-modal comparisons), which involves not only consistency of definitions, but also consistency, or at least similarity, among design features and data collection and processing procedures. As an example, the comparability of two data systems may be affected by differences in the method of data collection (such as personal interview, telephone interview, self-report, abstracting information from administrative reports, and obtaining data from such recording or sensing equipment as highway sensors). (See Box 3-1 for examples of lack of comparability of data for a single transportation mode and for cross-modal analysis.)

---

[1]The two attributes should not be viewed as totally distinct. Indeed, relevance may be said to encompass quality in that relevance means broadly the usefulness of a data set for an application, and data of poor quality are hardly useful even if they provide relevant information in other respects. However, the requirements (e.g., staff skills) for addressing data quality as distinct from the other substantive dimensions of relevance differ, so that it makes sense to discuss data quality and relevance as separate attributes.

[2]The discussion draws on the thinking among statistical agencies in the United States and elsewhere. See, for example, Australian Bureau of Statistics (1990); Bureau of Economic Analysis (1995); Statistics Canada (1992); and Statistics Sweden (1994).

BOX 3-1
Comparability Issues for Transportation Data: Examples

1. The Definition of "Fatality" Across Transportation Modes

Until recently, modal administrations in USDOT used different definitions of a transportation-related "fatality." The definition of a highway fatality was any death that resulted from and occurred within 30 days of a motor vehicle accident. The definition of a railroad fatality was any death that resulted from and occurred within 365 days of a railroad or grade-crossing accident or any death of a railroad employee from occupational illness within 365 days after the illness was diagnosed by a physician. Still other definitions were in use in the department. In May 1994, the secretary of transportation required all modal administrations to use the 30-day definition of a transportation fatality (Bureau of Transportation Statistics, *National Transportation Statistics 1996*:95).

2. Alternate Estimates of Motor Vehicles

"There is a lack of consensus on the number of motor vehicles operated in the United States and the distance those vehicles operate. Most commonly cited motor vehicle statistics . . . are provided by the states to the Federal Highway Administration and published in *Highway Statistics*. The National Highway Traffic Safety Administration uses alternate numbers from R.L. Polk, Inc. . . . The Bureau of the Census also used R.L. Polk data for the Truck Inventory and Use Survey" (Bureau of Transportation Statistics, *Transportation Statistics Annual Report 1996*:110).

3. Alternative Criteria for Reporting Highway Accidents

"Different states use different criteria to determine when police are required to report accidents involving only property damage. Most states use vehicle damage costs as the primary criterion. Damage thresholds vary significantly, however, ranging from $50 in Arkansas and the District of Columbia to $1,000 in Colorado" (Bureau of Transportation Statistics, *Transportation Statistics Annual Report 1996*:82).

4. Measures of Risk Exposure Across Transportation Modes

"Many different types of exposure measures . . . are used to analyze accident statistics. There is disagreement, however, about which best measures crash risk. Furthermore, the available measures of risk exposure may differ from one mode to the next . . . . For example, if vehicle-miles-traveled is the measure of risk exposure for highway crashes and the number of hours flown is the measure used for general aviation accidents, how will we compare safety trends between the two modes?" (Bureau of Transportation Statistics, *Transportation Statistics Annual Report 1996*:83).

- *Accuracy or bias*, which in general concerns how well a set of estimates approximates the true values of the phenomena under study and specifically concerns errors that are due to systematic mismeasurement.[3] Sources of systematic bias may include:
  — differential coverage of groups in the population being studied (e.g., research has documented undercoverage of minorities in the decennial census and household surveys and of smaller establishments in surveys of businesses and farms);
  — differential nonresponse by reporting units (e.g., lower response rates to surveys for working families who are harder to find at home, underreporting of accidents that involve minor injuries or property damage);
  — missing or erroneous reporting of specific items that is linked with other characteristics (e.g., higher missing data rates in surveys for income and assets on the part of people with high incomes);
  — biases in imputation and other data editing procedures that attempt to correct for missing data and other reporting errors.
- *Variability*, which includes instability in estimates from the use of a sample and from other sources. For example, variability may stem from differences in how stringently enumerators or other data collectors apply specified procedures or from the variable application of editing and imputation procedures.
- *Extent of revisions* in time series, due to supplementation of preliminary data with later reports and other factors (see Young, 1996).

Statistical agencies have developed tools to measure some of the above aspects of data quality. Effective application of these tools requires that there be a technical staff engaged in ongoing methodological work to measure data quality and to develop design features for data systems that can provide users with evidence about quality. (See discussion below in the section on "Staffing.")

A focus on documenting, evaluating, and improving data quality along the above dimensions is a central mission of a statistical agency. Such a focus is particularly important for BTS because data collection is so widely dispersed in the transportation field, making it difficult for users to assess the comparability, accuracy, and variability of data programs across the various transportation modes and a variety of public and private data sources.

We did not ourselves conduct a review of the quality of transportation data programs, and hence we cannot say whether they have serious data quality problems. However, no set of data is without error, and every data program has quality problems to a greater or lesser degree. What is important for a statistical

---

[3]A more technical definition is that estimates have low bias if they tend to be equal to the true values on average when the sampling process (or other data collection procedure) is repeated many times.

agency like BTS is to document the errors and other problems in data programs in its area and to assess the extent to which they compromise the use of the data for their intended purposes. On the basis of documentation and evaluation, the agency should identify priority data programs for improvement, taking account of the need for the data and the costs and feasibility of improvement, and should implement a phased effort to effect improvements as resources are available.

All that is not to say that data documentation, evaluation, and improvement efforts are not being carried out appropriately and well for particular transportation data programs, such as particular surveys and administrative reporting systems. However, data improvement activities for a particular data program do not ensure that the data will be comparable or of comparable quality when used with data from other programs, which is likely to be necessary to perform analyses across transportation modes or across time. Indeed, the Transportation Research Board report, *Data for Decisions* (National Research Council, 1992a), emphasized the problems with cross-modal comparisons.

BTS has highlighted some issues of cross-modal comparability in its *Transportation Statistics Annual Reports* (see Box 3-1). However, our review of its programs and data products and services indicates that BTS to date has not focused sufficient attention on helping users understand the problems of available transportation data nor on developing a systematic program to evaluate and improve the quality of transportation data (see sections below on "Documentation" and "Data Evaluation and Improvement;" see also Appendixes D and E). Such a program will require not only that BTS address data programs that it operates directly, but also that it work collaboratively with statistical units in other modal administrations in USDOT and with other data providers to ensure a focus on the quality of transportation data.

Given limited budgets, it is rarely possible to improve the quality of a data system on all dimensions nor to improve both quality and relevance to the same extent: statistical agencies are commonly faced with making choices or trade-offs among them. For example, without increasing total costs, it may be difficult to increase the sample size of a survey in order to reduce sampling variability and at the same time devote efforts to reduce undercoverage of people or establishments. Similarly, it may be difficult to increase sample size and at the same time maintain the desired frequency of data collection (an aspect of relevance). An important function of a statistical agency is to make these trade-offs on the basis of the best assessment possible of currently available data and the likely payoffs to investments in them. Looking to the future, the increasing capabilities of computer-assisted data collection and the combined uses of administrative and survey data may make it feasible in some instances to achieve simultaneous cost and burden reductions and improvements in data quality and relevance. Statistical agencies need to keep abreast of these developments and integrate them into their work. A prerequisite for BTS to undertake these activities is that it build strong statistical and analytical capabilities in its staff.

STAFFING

The 1991 ISTEA envisions BTS as a statistical agency for USDOT that provides leadership to the department in such areas as developing data quality standards, working with the other modal administrations and the states to develop indicators of the transportation system, coordinating collection of transportation data by USDOT with other federal agencies, and improving the quality and relevance of transportation data for cross-modal, system-wide analysis. To take on these leadership roles, and in particular to enhance the department's focus on data quality, BTS must have adequate technical and analytical expertise on its staff. Such expertise is essential for BTS to document, evaluate, and improve its own data systems and data products. In turn, excellence in its own operations is a prerequisite for the agency to acquire the stature and moral authority that are necessary for BTS to become credible in a leadership role for the department as a whole.

At present, BTS is a small agency; it lacks the depth and breadth of statistical and methodological expertise on its staff to coordinate a comprehensive program for USDOT of documenting, evaluating, and improving the department's data or, more generally, to provide statistical advice to other units.[4] A key element in BTS's future evolution as a statistical agency will be its ability to develop the necessary capabilities on its staff. BTS's progress in this regard will become even more important to the extent that budget pressures on the other modal administrations in USDOT constrain their ability to maintain statistical and analytical expertise in their agencies.

Current and Planned Staffing

The current BTS staff (37 people as of fall 1996, of which 16 were in the Office of Airline Information) have expertise and experience in a wide range of fields. A number of staff have backgrounds in transportation research, geographic information systems, data technology, and other relevant fields. However, few staff have extensive expertise in statistical methods (e.g., sampling, estimation, survey research and evaluation). Plans to fill 23 authorized vacancies include two mid-level positions for a mathematical statistician and a survey statistician. (These positions were recently filled.)

---

[4] As an example of an area in which BTS could provide technical assistance if it had sufficient staff capability, the Federal Aviation Administration was recently faced with the question of whether it could rank the safety records of individual air carriers. This question involves such statistical issues as the appropriate choice of safety indicators (e.g., number of accidents with fatalities per million aircraft-miles flown, number of accidents with fatalities per 100,000 takeoffs, number of fatalities per million passenger-miles flown) and whether differences among those indicators for individual airlines are meaningful (i.e., relate to factors that are under the airlines' control, such as age and maintenance of equipment, versus such factors as weather patterns at the airports used most by an airline).

An earlier staffing plan, which envisioned a total of about 75 staff after filling vacancies, included a position of senior adviser for statistical policy in the BTS director's office. BTS was directed by the Office of the Secretary to reduce its authorized full-time-equivalent (FTE) staff from 75 to 60 people. In revising its staffing plan, BTS chose to drop the senior statistical adviser position, which was slotted for a GS-15 level (the top grade below the Senior Executive Service), and to share statistical oversight responsibilities among the director, deputy director, and two associate directors. (The director is a presidential appointee; the deputy director and associate directors are Senior Executive Service positions.) The reason given for this decision, which BTS hopes to reverse if it is authorized to have more FTE staff, is that it is difficult to justify positions at the GS-15 level, particularly under strictures from the current administration, as part of its Reinventing Government initiative, to reduce the ratio of senior supervisors to other staff.

Building a Strong Statistical Staff

In the panel's view, it is essential for BTS to implement a staffing plan that gives much higher priority to building expertise in statistical methods and related quantitative fields than is provided in the current staffing plan. Needed areas of skill include statistical sampling, statistical design, cognitive foundations of survey measurement, advanced data collection methods, editing, imputation for missing data, and statistical estimation from complex sample surveys. At present, BTS's statistical staff capabilities are augmented by Census Bureau staff who work on the Commodity Flow Survey and the American Travel Survey. However, there is no substitute for sufficient in-house staff with the necessary expertise if BTS is to achieve excellence in its own operations and if it is to be able to exercise statistical leadership for the department as a whole.[5] BTS should reprogram a portion of the available vacancies to emphasize statistical and related skills and should move expeditiously to fill those vacancies.

To underscore the importance of a strong in-house statistical staff for BTS and to provide a focal point for BTS's work to evaluate and improve the quality of transportation data, the panel believes that BTS should be authorized by the department to appoint an associate director for statistical methods and research at the Senior Executive Service level (see recommendation 2 at the end of the chapter). The senior level is justified given the importance for a statistical agency of

---

[5]Many statistical agencies, like BTS, use contractor staff for a variety of purposes, including data collection and processing, programming support for analytical work, conference arrangements, and publication preparation. We did not consider in detail the appropriate mix of in-house and contractor staff for a statistical agency—many factors enter into the choice of mix, including costs, constraints on full-time-equivalent staff, and past agency experience. However, we stress that a statistical agency must have sufficient in-house statistical and technical capability to carry out key functions and properly direct the work of contractors.

keeping abreast of and applying advanced statistical methods and techniques to such functions as data evaluation and improvement. Although the titles vary, other major statistical agencies, such as the Census Bureau, the National Center for Education Statistics, and the National Center for Health Statistics, have similar positions.

The BTS associate director for statistical methods and research should have extensive expertise in such areas as statistical estimation and survey research methods. BTS should authorize the associate director to build a statistical staff that plays a leadership role for BTS in developing data quality standards, designing and implementing evaluation studies of BTS data systems, and conducting research on improved methods of data collection, processing, and estimation. The BTS statistical staff would take the lead in working with statistical units in the other USDOT modal administrations to develop standards and priorities for data documentation, evaluation, and improvement of the department's data systems. The BTS statistical staff would also provide technical assistance to the other modal administrations as appropriate.

The associate director for statistical methods and research and BTS as a whole could benefit from outside statistical advice on a regular basis. As required by the 1991 ISTEA, BTS currently has an Advisory Council on Transportation Statistics, which meets twice a year to discuss BTS's programs and review new initiatives. This group has a strong user orientation and focuses on issues regarding the kinds of transportation data that are needed for important policy purposes. A separate advisory group that focuses on issues of statistical methods and standards would also be very useful.

As some other statistical agencies have done (e.g., the Bureau of Justice Statistics, the Census Bureau, the Energy Information Administration), BTS could ask the American Statistical Association to establish a working group of experts to meet regularly with its statistical staff on technical matters. The members of such a group should have expertise in such areas as sampling and survey design, advanced data collection methods, weighting and imputation methods for missing and erroneous data, and statistical estimation from complex sample surveys. As BTS develops closer working relationships with the other modal administrations, many of which have large amounts of data collected from administrative reporting systems in addition to sample surveys, a statistical advisory group should also include experts in the design and statistical applications of administrative records. Such a group could assist BTS to evaluate alternative designs and data collection, processing, and analysis procedures for surveys and other data collection programs and to establish priorities for statistical research and evaluation.

Continuing Staff Development

Building and maintaining strong statistical and technical staff capabilities requires an agency's continuing attention. BTS's top management should give priority to identifying opportunities for staff development and to encouraging staff to take full advantage of them. Among the kinds of activities that can foster the development of technical skills are attendance at advanced courses, presentations at professional association meetings, and publication in professional journals.

BTS already has some useful vehicles for staff development in place. Its new peer-reviewed publication, the *Journal of Transportation and Statistics*, should prove to be a valuable means by which to stimulate methodological research and analysis on the part of staff. Also, its regular seminar series, which brings leading transportation researchers from the United States and abroad to present analytical results and discuss important issues for transportation policy, is an important means of enhancing professional knowledge and skills. This program should be continued and expanded to include relevant issues of statistical methods and approach.

Some statistical agencies have specified goals for the performance of technical staff that relate to keeping current in the technical developments of their field. These goals can be achieved by participation in relevant graduate courses at local universities, attendance at continuing education short courses, or attendance at other seminars that are relevant to the field. There are several active programs in the Washington, D.C., area that provide opportunities for professional development of these kinds. By placing explicit direction in performance plans for continuous improvement of technical skills, the agency can make explicit its commitment to this goal.

Some other ways to enhance professional capabilities are more costly and hence may be appropriate for BTS to consider only when it is somewhat larger and has more resources. For example, several statistical agencies have visiting fellows programs that are administered through the American Statistical Association, in which distinguished statisticians and other researchers come to the agency for a specified time period to work on topics of mutual interest. The visiting fellows gain insights into the practical operational problems of a statistical agency, and the agency staff benefit from working closely with leading researchers. Such a program involves significant budget commitments and can also take time to become established. It may be difficult for a small agency such as BTS to accomplish, but the concept is worth investigating for possible implementation at a future date.

Similarly, statistical agencies sometimes provide their staff with opportunities to work at other agencies or organizations for periods of 6 to 18 months in areas that will benefit the home agency. When BTS is larger, it could consider occasionally detailing one or two people to another statistical unit within USDOT, to another federal statistical agency, or to another organization with statistical expertise, as a way for staff to gain valuable experiences and insights. Similarly, BTS could sponsor staff from other USDOT modal administrations or other federal statistical agencies to work at BTS. Exchanges of staff between BTS and other statistical units within USDOT could be particularly valuable in building cooperative relationships, cross-modal perspectives, and a strong commitment to data quality within the department.

QUALITY STANDARDS

For documenting, evaluating, and improving data quality, it is very helpful for a statistical agency to develop explicit notions of appropriate standards for collecting, processing, and publishing the data. BTS has been working with other USDOT modal administrations to develop improved means of data dissemination, such as more user-friendly CD-ROM formats, which is a step toward facilitating systematic data analysis. BTS has not yet begun to work with the other modal administrations to develop guidelines for data quality throughout USDOT, as it is mandated to do by the 1991 ISTEA, nor to standardize key concepts, definitions, and procedures to the extent feasible and appropriate in order to facilitate cross-modal analysis.

In some people's interpretations, BTS is constrained from moving in this direction by the provision in the 1991 ISTEA that nothing in the legislation shall be construed "(1) to authorize the Bureau to require any other department or agency to collect data; or (2) to reduce the authority of any other officer of the Department of Transportation to collect and disseminate data independently." However, our view is that this provision does not contradict the mandate for BTS to develop guidelines for data quality for USDOT in collaboration with statistical units in the other modal administrations.

Indeed, we urge that the reauthorization of BTS strengthen its role by requiring it to develop data quality standards, consistent with good statistical practice, that are binding throughout USDOT and available for use by transportation agencies outside USDOT and for reference by the public (see recommendation 3 at the end of the chapter). In so doing, Congress will both underscore the importance of focusing on the quality of transportation data and clarify BTS's responsibility to move forward in this area.

BTS should develop data quality standards for the department with the cooperation and input of the other statistical units in USDOT obtained through a department-wide standards committee that is chaired by the BTS director. Cooperative efforts are essential, so that the other units can come to see the benefits to their users and buy into the process and so that BTS can carry out its leadership function in this area as a facilitator and not as a regulator or enforcer. The standards committee should be mandated in the reauthorization of BTS.

The reauthorization should also require that BTS every 2 years prepare a report to the Congress that describes progress during the previous 2 years to set standards and that identifies improvements in data quality by BTS and other USDOT statistical units and in the provision of information about quality to data users. We recommend the biennial report primarily as a tool to promote a focus on data quality; it could also usefully describe major steps to improve the relevance of transportation data in terms of timeliness, subject matter and geographic detail, appropriateness of concepts and definitions, and the initiation of new data programs or the consolidation or elimination of data programs in order to satisfy users' priority needs more cost-effectively.

We specify a biennial rather than annual report so that there is time for progress to be made and for the report to be a substantive document and not simply a time-consuming exercise in fulfilling a requirement. Another way to ensure substance is for each report to identify selected data programs or subject areas in which quality improvements will be sought on a priority basis and to highlight those areas in the next report, commenting more generally on other areas.

The biennial report that we recommend is not to be confused with the *Transportation Statistics Annual Report*s that are mandated by the 1991 ISTEA. Those reports have regularly included a section on the state of transportation statistics, but those sections have been general in nature and do not meet the need we see for reporting improvements on specific quality dimensions for specific transportation data programs or sets of related programs. We discuss the role of the *Transportation Statistics Annual Reports* in providing needed time series indicators and analyses of transportation trends in Chapter 4, where we suggest that there may be more cost-effective ways of providing these kinds of information than the current prescribed format.

We recognize that BTS is still a new, small agency within the U.S. Department of Transportation with a challenging array of responsibilities. Also, as discussed earlier, BTS currently lacks the staff resources and the necessary technical capabilities and expertise with which to develop its statistical functions as fully as its data compilation and dissemination functions. Hence, it will not be an easy task for BTS to assume responsibility for leading a process to develop quality standards for USDOT as a whole.

However, we believe strongly that BTS must evolve to be the statistical agency for USDOT that is envisioned in the 1991 ISTEA, which means that it must begin to take on a leadership role in several areas. The need for leadership to sort out higher- from lower-quality data and to identify priorities for new and improved data is clear from reviews of transportation data needs (e.g., National Research Council, 1992a). Such reviews invariably cite the large volume of data available from public and private sources but the lack of comparable data that provide useful *information* for analyses of important transportation issues, particularly those that require a cross-modal or system-wide perspective.

We recognize that progress in such areas as developing quality standards cannot happen overnight. Nonetheless, the work must begin, and the agency that was established to be the major statistical unit for the department as a whole must be given the authority and motivation to move forward collaboratively with the other statistical units in USDOT.

Types of Standards

The term "quality standards" can take on several different meanings, as discussed below. Statistical agencies may find it useful to develop standards that reflect more than one of these interpretations. Also, standards will usually apply to a range of activities, including data system design and development, data collection, data processing, and publication.

Standards as consistent definitions and protocols In this interpretation, standards setting involves the development of consistent definitions of key concepts and variables in order to permit comparisons and statistical aggregation. Examples are standard industrial and occupational classifications for the reporting of economic data, standard accounting concepts and fiscal years for the reporting of financial data by governmental units and business enterprises, and base years for indices.

The importance of work on standard definitions for transportation concepts to permit cross-modal analysis is clear. Indeed, to date, this is the single area of standards setting that BTS has considered for its future agenda, although there are other equally important areas. BTS has taken the very first step in this area (in its publication, *Transportation Expressions*) by documenting the various definitions used in transportation data systems for such concepts as "semitrailer" and "fatality." It has also addressed in general terms some of the problems for data use caused by the lack of common definitions in some areas (in its *Transportation Statistics Annual Reports*—see Box 3-1 for examples). However, much more needs to be done to evaluate for users the implications of different definitions for cross-modal analyses and then to work to standardize key definitions.[6]

Standards as definitions of minimum acceptable quality In this interpretation, standards serve as performance criteria for data collection and publication. For example, for a household or business survey, a statistical agency may set a standard for a minimally acceptable final response rate from the sampled units, such as 75 or 85 percent, and set aside funds to be used for additional follow-up efforts if the initial data collection efforts fall short of obtaining the specified standard.[7] Many statistical agencies have minimum publication standards for the reporting of survey estimates: for example, differences across time or population groups will not be reported in summaries of findings if they fall below specified criteria

---

[6]Striving for comparability of key concepts and definitions must be undertaken carefully. In some instances, comparability may not be feasible, except by moving to a least common denominator in which importance nuances are blurred or lost.

[7]For example, one agency's standards manual (Energy Information Administration, no date) specifies a minimum final response rate of 75 percent of eligible respondents, covering 85 percent of anticipated aggregates (e.g., total sales volume for regions). Determining an appropriate response rate standard also requires defining the term (who is an "eligible" respondent, whether the calculation is made using weights, etc.).

for statistical significance; estimates will not be published if they are based on fewer than a specified number of reporting units. Another minimum acceptable quality standard may involve time between completion of data collection and publication: for example, the Bureau of Labor Statistics and the Bureau of the Census commit to completing data collection and publication of the monthly unemployment statistics within a few weeks of the reference week for the estimates.

The use of minimum acceptable quality standards is desirable when there is strong evidence linking the standard to the utility of the data. For example, the survey research literature provides substantial evidence that survey nonrespondents are likely to differ from respondents in important ways for which editing and imputation are not likely to compensate (see, e.g., Jabine, King, and Petroni, 1990). Hence, there is justification for establishing a high standard for a minimally acceptable final response rate to a survey in order to minimize bias from nonresponse. As another example, the suppression of publication of estimates that do not meet minimum precision thresholds simplifies use of statistical publications. Readers are assured that all estimates presented meet a specified level of reliability.

Many USDOT data systems are based on administrative records that represent censuses of the relevant reporting units and not surveys, so that minimum publication standards involving statistical confidence levels or sample sizes are not applicable. (Examples are the Fatal Accident Reporting System of the National Highway Traffic Safety Administration, the National Bridge Inventory of the Federal Highway Administration, various administrative databases of the Federal Aviation Administration, and operational and financial data on certificated U.S. air carriers of the Office of Airline Information in BTS.)[8] However, there can be reporting problems in administrative data systems (e.g., failure to report selected items or to provide any information at all, errors in reporting due to data transmission problems or the use of nonstandard definitions) that may, in some instances, merit the development of a minimum acceptable standard below which data will not be released.

Standards as protocols to reveal indicators of the quality of published statistical information In this use of standards, there is a commitment to identify key indicators of data quality and to publish them as a matter of standard practice in order to inform data users about limitations and problems in the data. (Agencies with this type of standard may or may not also establish minimum acceptable quality

---

[8]Some data programs in USDOT represent samples of administrative records for which statistical sampling considerations apply (e.g., the Carload Waybill sample of information provided by Class I freight railroads for a 1 percent sample of rail waybills, which the Federal Railroad Administration uses to analyze traffic patterns and competitiveness issues; the General Estimates System of the National Highway Traffic Safety Administration, which contains information on a sample of police-reported traffic crashes; and the Passenger Origin and Destination Survey of the Office of Airline Information in BTS, which contains information from a 10 percent sample of airline tickets).

standards.) Thus, for surveys, agencies may commit to publishing such quality indicators as sampling variability, response rates, missing data rates, response variance indicators, and comparisons to other similar data series. For administrative records-based data systems, agencies may commit to publishing such quality indicators as missing data rates and to describe differences in reporting practices across reporting units (e.g., differences in fiscal years for state or local government financial reports of highway revenues and expenditures).

Standards as methods of quality improvement In this interpretation, agencies use a set of quality indicators, such as those developed for publication (e.g., response rates, item nonreporting rates), as the basis for setting and tracking data improvement goals. For example, an agency might set a goal of reducing nonresponse rates by a specified amount for key survey items by experimenting with questionnaire design and question wording. As another example, an agency might set a goal that, over a specified time period, all reporting units for an administrative records data system, such as state and local governments, will convert to common definitions of key concepts or to common practices for data reporting.

Standards as hortatory statements of practice In this interpretation, agencies issue guidelines or statements of best practice on dimensions of quality (e.g., timeliness, low variability) and seek to nurture aspirations to those practices. However, they do not attempt to enforce minimum acceptable standards.

Standards-Setting Practices

The utility of standards is that they are tools to achieve data quality; all of the alternative kinds of standards described above can play a role in achieving high-quality data. A new statistical agency faces unusual problems in setting standards and striving for quality. It may easily fail if it merely adopts the practices of mature agencies.

BTS has yet to develop a culture that places prime importance on the continuous improvement of data quality. The agency can, however, shape its culture in that direction. In an agency that is attempting to build a culture of commitment to quality improvement, the construction of formal written standards for the publication of estimates and for minimal acceptable data quality can act as a catalyst to communicate to wide audiences the importance of data quality to the mission of the agency. Written standards can thus serve both to define an internal spirit in this direction and to define the image of the organization to the larger world.

Established statistical agencies vary in the types of standards they have developed and in how they achieve compliance with quality standards (see U.S. Department of Education, 1988, which reviews the practices of the Bureau of Justice Statistics, the Bureau of Labor Statistics, the Census Bureau, the Energy Information Administration, and the National Center for Health Statistics in the areas of standards setting, quality control, and tabulation and publication review).

In many long-standing statistical agencies, there are no written standards; the agency believes that the existing organizational culture enforces adherence to a high level of professionalism in carrying out data collection and analysis programs. Newer statistical agencies that contract for data collection with outside organizations more often have written standards (see, e.g., Energy Information Administration, no date; for other examples of written standards, see Flemming, 1992; Freedman et al., 1987; Sirken et al., 1992). In some agencies, there are units with review authority for quality standards: these units must review tabulations and analyses before they are released, with the possibility that the work must be redone if minimum acceptable standards are not met.

There are advantages and disadvantages to each of these practices of achieving high standards of data quality. On one hand, written standards can be heavy-handed and make it difficult for agencies to experiment with new methods for data collection, processing, and publication. On the other hand, the absence of written standards means that agencies must have very well-developed systems for training, mentoring, and evaluating their own and contractor staff. In the early years of a statistical agency, it may be necessary to construct written standards in order to develop, at a later stage, an organizational culture that inherently promotes data quality and relevance.

Considerations for BTS

BTS will need to think through appropriate uses and meanings of quality standards. For its own use, we suggest that BTS develop minimum acceptable quality standards for data from its survey and other data collection programs, commit to publishing specific quality indicators and other kinds of documentation for those data, and plan to use these indicators to guide continuing efforts toward data improvement. For some programs, it may be the case that not enough is known to publish certain kinds of quality indicators (e.g., indicators of various reporting errors). In those instances, it will be important to identify priority areas for evaluation studies that can provide input for more complete documentation and suggest subsequent work to improve data quality.

At the same time that BTS is developing its own quality standards, it should be working with other statistical units in USDOT as recommended earlier to develop quality standards for the department as a whole. It will clearly be important to work on standardizing definitions and other aspects of data systems for the department, to the extent feasible and appropriate, that can facilitate cross-modal and system-wide analyses of transportation data sets on a comparable basis. Such work will be challenging and will require identification of priority areas to address, given the large number of transportation issue areas and data systems.

There may also be some minimum acceptable quality standards that are appropriate to develop for the department, such as pretesting requirements for new survey instruments and reporting forms. However, we do not suggest focusing on the development of minimum acceptable quality standards, both because of the wide range of transportation data programs and because of the importance of nurturing collaborative and not adversarial relationships of BTS with the other modal administrations.

What seems to us feasible and desirable to develop is a set of quality indicators and other information that BTS and all of the USDOT modal administrations commit to publish about their data in statistical reports and documentation of data sets—that is, not standards for the data themselves but publication standards that inform users about data limitations and, over time, serve to guide the development of improved data. The minimum acceptable set of quality indicators in reports and documentation will vary by type of data system and type of report. For example, estimates of sampling variability are essential to provide for estimates that derive from a survey, but they do not apply for estimates from a census (although there may be other sources of variation that should be documented). Also, it will generally be appropriate to publish fewer quality indicators in brief summaries or abstracts of data systems than in full-blown reports that present detailed tables and analyses or in documentation of data sets; however, even the briefest summary or abstract should include basic quality indicators (see section on "Documenting Data Quality" below; see also Flemming, 1992).

In order to carry out a strengthened mandate to establish binding data quality standards for USDOT (whether publication standards, consistent definitions, or minimum acceptable quality standards), BTS in collaboration with the department-wide standards committee recommended earlier will need to develop explicit written standards in most instances. However, we caution against rigidifying standards or setting up an office within BTS that is viewed as having a police function. BTS and the other statistical units in USDOT should work together to develop standards and periodically review and revise them to keep the standards relevant to new methodology for data collection, processing, and publication and to changing transportation data needs. BTS and the other statistical units should also collaborate to prepare the biennial report recommended earlier that describes progress in documenting and improving the quality of transportation data in USDOT. Such a report can be much more than an exercise in meeting a legislative requirement. If well done, it can identify priority areas for data improvement and generally contribute to an ongoing quality assurance function for the department's data systems.

DOCUMENTING DATA QUALITY

Setting standards is an important and challenging function of a statistical agency but, to be useful, the standards must be applied in documenting, evaluating, and improving the quality of the data in the agency's subject area. Statistical agencies face daunting tasks in these areas. The question for BTS is where to begin.

To date, BTS has concentrated on letting users know about the vast array of existing transportation data sources and making it convenient for them to obtain data through its World Wide Web site and other modes of dissemination. With this goal in mind, BTS has not attempted any type of screening or gatekeeping of the data it assembles for redistribution, nor has it made an effort to distinguish the quality or usefulness of particular data sources. It has also not yet begun to evaluate available data systematically nor to lay out a program of improvement of key transportation data sets. The result is that users now have access to a large volume of information of varying quality with no roadmap to assist them in understanding the limitations and appropriate uses of particular data sets.

We believe that BTS should now begin to focus more on data quality than on quantity. It should place high priority on the development of more complete information for users about the methods of data collection, error measurement, definitional comparability across data sets, and other dimensions of quality of the transportation data that it makes available (see recommendation 4 at the end of the chapter). Because of the importance of cross-modal analysis and because of BTS's mandate in this area, information provided to users should include how data for one transportation mode relate (or do not relate) to data for other modes. Such efforts at documentation will identify aspects of data systems about which little is known and for which evaluation is needed and help set priorities for evaluation studies that can ultimately lead to initiatives for data improvement.

Simply to expand the available documentation will require setting priorities and making choices. BTS should begin by ensuring that documentary materials for the data systems that BTS itself sponsors are complete and meet high standards, as discussed above. It should then identify topic areas that are of particular policy importance and work with relevant agencies inside and outside USDOT to develop the most appropriate documentation. (For data systems for which good documentation already exists, BTS should highlight the appropriate references on its web site and in its directory of transportation data sources and other relevant publications.) Below we discuss documentation concerns for BTS's own data systems and then give examples of improvements that BTS could make in the short term to its key publications and web site to help users understand the limitations and uses of other available data sets.

Documentation of BTS Data

BTS currently sponsors two major surveys about intermodal transport of people and goods—the Commodity Flow Survey (CFS) and the American Travel Survey (ATS). The Census Bureau cosponsors and collects the CFS data as part of the economic census program conducted every 5 years; it also collects the ATS data under contract from BTS. (Current plans are to conduct the ATS every 5 years as well.)

The Census Bureau has released a series of reports from the CFS (see, e.g.,

Bureau of the Census, 1996a), which include information about the data, reflecting the Census Bureau's long-standing practice and standards in this area. Each report provides a description of the survey and the data collection and estimation methods used, definitions of variables, assessments of comparability with previous surveys and data reliability (including estimates of sampling variability), and a copy of the questionnaire. Although extensive, the documentation does not answer some important questions: for example, there is no information on nonresponse rates by shippers to the survey. Also, the documentation does not address analytical uses of the data that are appropriate given what is known about the data quality.

BTS could usefully develop examples of appropriate applications of the CFS data for system-wide transportation policy analysis, including examples of analysis of trends over time from comparisons with earlier rounds of the CFS, to the extent feasible. Materials that guide the states in appropriate use of the CFS data could also be very helpful (see discussion of technical assistance to the states in Chapter 4). Developing such materials will require that BTS staff themselves become expert users of the CFS data, which, in turn, is one of the best ways for a statistical agency to evaluate the quality of a data set and to determine needed improvements in both data and documentation. Assuming that future rounds of the CFS continue to be cosponsored with the Census Bureau, BTS should become an active partner in planning and reviewing the accompanying informational materials.

Data from the 1995 ATS are not yet available. However, in contrast to the CFS, the ATS reports that will be released shortly will be BTS publications and not Census Bureau publications. BTS should give careful attention to the type and extent of documentation that is provided with the reports and with computer-readable data products from the ATS. Important information to include is a discussion of comparability of the 1995 ATS and the 1995 and earlier rounds of the Nationwide Personal Transportation Survey (NPTS) and of how the two data sets can be used together for analysis purposes. (The 1995 ATS covered trips of 75 or more miles by a sample of 80,000 households over the course of a year; the 1995 NPTS covered a day's worth of trips together with longer trips over a two-week period for a considerably smaller sample of 22,000 households.)

Microdata will be available from the ATS; microdata are also available from the NPTS.[9] Complex microdata products require extensive documentation so that users can analyze the data with full understanding of the meaning of the variables and structure of the data file. Such documentation should include not only a codebook, which provides essential information on locations and codes of

---

[9]The ATS and NPTS microdata files protect the confidentiality of responses from individual people and households by several methods, such as coding place of residence to broad geographic areas. Protecting the confidentiality of business respondents is more difficult (e.g., because of significant variation in such characteristics as size); hence, microdata files are not available from the CFS.

variables, but also a user's guide, which typically includes information on the survey design, the structure of the microdata set (e.g., if there are multiple types of records), limitations of the data and cautions for analysts, detailed definitions of variables, how to construct estimates of sampling error, comparability with related data sets, and the like (see, e.g., Bureau of the Census, 1991, 1992).

Finally, it is important to document the results of evaluation studies of complex, ongoing data collection systems, such as the ATS and CFS, in a way that highlights their implications for appropriate use of the data and that identifies areas for future improvement. One approach is to develop and periodically update a quality profile, which brings together all that is known about the sources and extent of error—nonsampling error as well as sampling error—that may affect the estimates from a survey or other data system (see, e.g., Energy Information Administration, 1996; Jabine, 1994; Jabine, King, and Petroni, 1990).

Another approach is to put out a methods bulletin every 2-3 years with chapters on all of the data collection programs in an agency, reviewing for each the survey design, collection and processing methods, and whatever is known about the error and quality of the estimates (see, e.g., Bureau of Labor Statistics, 1992). A methods bulletin is readily updated—individual chapters can be expanded as more is learned about particular data programs. The Bureau of Economic Analysis has begun to develop a methods bulletin for its estimates with a series of articles in the *Survey of Current Business* that will be combined into a single document.

In addition to developing quality profiles or chapters in a methods bulletin series for the ATS and CFS, BTS should immediately begin to use its planned *Journal of Transportation and Statistics* as an outlet for publishing methodological papers about its surveys (subject to peer review). BTS should also encourage staff of statistical units in other USDOT modal administrations to publish methodological papers about their own data systems in the journal and should investigate the possibility of joint articles with staff from other statistical agencies on issues of mutual interest.

Documentation of Other Data

BTS's work with the other USDOT modal administrations to develop standards for data documentation will ultimately lead to more consistent and complete information for users about the quality of the department's data systems and how they can be used for cross-modal, system-wide analyses. At this stage, BTS must necessarily accept the documentation that other agencies provide for data that they furnish to BTS to disseminate in statistical compendia, CD-ROMs, and via the BTS web site. Yet there are modest steps that BTS can take now to emphasize for transportation data producers and users the importance of focusing on data quality.

Directory of Transportation Data Sources

BTS's directory is a helpful basic reference document for users to learn about available transportation data. The number of entries has approximately doubled from the first edition in December 1993 to the 1996 edition (see Table 2-1), and the directory now covers data sets from USDOT agencies, other federal agencies, the United Nations, state governments, private organizations, Canada, and Mexico. The information provided for each data set (report, CD-ROM, data tape) includes:

- title;
- mode of transportation;
- brief abstract;
- source of data;
- geographic coverage;
- time span, when first developed, update frequency, last update;
- file attributes if applicable (e.g., number of records);
- significant features or limitations;
- corresponding print source;
- sponsoring and performing organization(s); and
- availability and contact for additional information.

Several additions would enhance the ability of the directory to focus users on data quality. For computer-readable data sets, BTS should add references to available documentation. For surveys, the abstract should provide not only the sample size, but also the response rate, both of which are important and easily conveyed indicators of quality. BTS should also increase the number of entries for which significant features or limitations are provided (many entries lack any information under this heading) and consider how to provide information on the suitability (or lack of suitability) of a data system for cross-modal analysis. Finally, in addition to a title index and an index by transportation mode, it would help users who want to find relevant data on a particular topic, such as safety, for the directory to include a subject index.

National Transportation Statistics **Compendium**

The annual *National Transportation Statistics (NTS)* reports are intended to serve the same reference function for transportation as the annual *Statistical Abstract of the United States* does for a wide range of subject areas—that is, to bring together a large number of data series in a single, regularly updated volume. The *NTS* reports provide historical trend data for all of the transportation modes on performance, safety, costs, energy use, and other topics, compiled from USDOT agencies and other sources. The 1996 volume includes 134 tables and 42 charts. (As in the *Statistical Abstract of the United States*, there is no analytical text in the *NTS* reports.)

However, the usefulness of the *NTS* reports is compromised by the lack of detailed explanatory notes, including those that would indicate significant changes in definitions across time and the implications of those changes for data comparability. Also lacking are explanatory materials that would help users understand the extent to which it is appropriate to compare data series on particular topics across transportation modes.

The *Statistical Abstract of the United States*, which includes many topics besides transportation, provides information on sampling and nonsampling errors for major data sources that is not found in the *NTS* reports, along with more extensive table notes for transportation data series than are found in the *NTS* reports. As an example, the *Statistical Abstract of the United States* (Bureau of the Census, 1996b:614) indicates the changes in the definition of Class I railroads since 1950 that were adopted by the Interstate Commerce Commission for regulatory purposes. The *NTS* provides the current definition, which is that a Class I railroad is one that has $250 million or more in operating revenues in 1992 dollars. However, it does not indicate historical changes: in 1950, Class I railroads were those with $4.5 million in operating revenues (1992 dollars); the threshold was revised 6 times in real dollar terms between 1950 and 1982. The 1996 *NTS* shows a pronounced decline in the number of Class I railroads from 1960 to 1994 and in the numbers of freight cars, employees, and miles of track owned by Class I railroads. Some portion of this decline is undoubtedly real—due to consolidation of rail companies, loss of business to trucking companies, and other factors. However, some portion of the decline may be an artifact of the definitional changes.

Finally, the *NTS* reports include numerous charts and graphs, many of which are useful in identifying important trends, but some of the charts need to be rethought in order to satisfy principles of good graphic design (see Cleveland, 1985, 1993; Tufte, 1983). Furthermore, reducing their number could free up space for material that explains and interprets key data series. In Appendix D, we use the section in the *1996 NTS* on airline safety to illustrate some of the kinds of changes that BTS should plan to make over the next few years, topic by topic, to improve the usefulness of the *NTS* volumes to help users understand the quality of the data and their appropriateness for cross-modal analysis.[10]

Data Products

BTS has released numerous data sets on CD-ROM, most of which were obtained from other agencies. One example is a CD-ROM of historical data from the National Highway Traffic Safety Administration's Fatal Accident Reporting System (FARS) and General Estimates System (GES). (FARS provides a census

---

[10]The *1997 NTS* reflects improvements in tables that anticipate some of the comments in Appendix D; it has no charts or graphs.

of traffic crashes that involve fatalities, and GES provides a probability sample of all police-reported traffic crashes.) Another example is a CD-ROM of data from the 1983 and 1990 Nationwide Personal Transportation Survey, sponsored by the Federal Highway Administration. BTS's Transportation Data Sampler CD-ROMs include selected reports, aggregate data sets, and microdata sets from a variety of sources. Documentation from the source agency is provided for data sets (e.g., the two NPTS files); however, it is not always clear which files contain documentation. For example, documentation for the Census Bureau's 1992 Truck Inventory and Use Survey on Transportation Data Sampler-3 is split among several files and not clearly identified for the user. Indeed, although the sampler has a brief description of each subdirectory that corresponds to a particular data system, it does not briefly describe each file within a subdirectory. The user has to hunt to find particular data sets and documentation.

Printed material that accompanies each CD-ROM should stress the importance of reviewing the documentation before accessing and using a data set. Also, either that material or an introductory document on the CD-ROM itself should provide a clear index, with brief annotations, to all of the files on the CD-ROM. In particular, the description should note whether the file is documentation or data and, if the latter, whether the file contains microdata for individual reporting units (households, accidents, establishments, etc.) or whether the data are aggregated in some manner. Microdata are more useful than aggregate data for detailed analyses and research, but they can be more difficult to use.

Finally, BTS should begin a program of reviewing documentation that is provided for data sets to determine if it contains minimum essential information and, if not, hold up data release until the needed information is added. For this purpose, BTS should be able to draw on the many existing examples of documentation standards (see, e.g., Flemming, 1992; Sirken et al., 1992) to develop a working set of minimum acceptable standards in advance of the final set of standards that is developed for the department as a whole.

Web Site

The BTS web site (see Figure 2-1) is a vast cornucopia of material, including: descriptions of BTS data products and services; data from selected reports and files from BTS and other sources; reports, reference documents, and many other publications from a wide range of sources (in the National Transportation Library portion of the site—see Figure 2-2); and links to other agencies, including the USDOT modal administrations, other federal agencies, and private organizations with some connection to the transportation field. The amount of material that is accessible through the site is impressive. However, we have several concerns (discussed below) about the site's ability to help users locate high-quality data and understand their uses and limitations. Adding to our concern is the

FOCUSING ON DATA QUALITY 53

impression that the site is being built piecemeal with little thought given to an overall structure that reflects a data user perspective.[11]

National Transportation Library (NTL) By far the largest part of the BTS web site is the NTL, which has received praise from reference librarians in the transportation field and is well organized to help users find documents on a particular topic. Yet the NTL contains few data and little information about data that is available elsewhere. For example, the safety portion of the site has almost 200 entries, few of which provide relevant data—the documents provided include, among others, reports of the U.S. General Accounting Office on aviation safety issues, the marine safety manual of the U.S. Coast Guard, recommended emergency preparedness guidelines for rail transit systems, and bicycle helmet laws by state.

These and similar documents may serve a useful reference purpose. However, we question the wisdom of devoting resources and staff attention to expand the NTL if that means fewer resources with which to improve the BTS web site as a guide to users about available data. There is also a problem that the quality of the documents may vary widely, and BTS has no way to control quality.[12]

Search capabilities for data The BTS web site can be confusing for the user who wants to find high-quality data (as opposed to reference documents) on a particular cross-modal topic, such as safety. The two sections of the site that provide data or descriptions of data are "Products" and "Databases." (Some BTS products also appear under "BTS Programs." The "Briefing Room" has a "Statistics" section, but it is limited to data on airline operations from the Office of Airline Information.)

The BTS "Products" section has a subject index in addition to an index by transportation mode; it is also searchable by the user (the search engine actually searches the entire site). However, the entries in the subject index are very general—for example, the *NTS* reports are listed as sources of safety data without further elaboration (see Figure 3-1).[13] A keyword search on "safety data" brings

---

[11]The BTS web site is updated frequently. Since we first began looking at the site in 1996, BTS has not only added new content, but also improved the organization of the site in several respects; however, more needs to be done. Our comments are based on the site as of April-June 1997.

[12]The NTL page carries a general disclaimer that inclusion of a document in the NTL "does not necessarily constitute endorsement" by BTS or USDOT (see Figure 2-2). BTS has also recently begun the use of automated software to check for documents in the NTL that are inaccessible because the site of the originating organization has been taken off the web or for another reason. The links for such documents will then be removed or corrected. (These kinds of problems can happen frequently: a review by our panel of the safety section of the NTL prior to the installation of regular checks found that almost two-fifths of the documents were inaccessible because the host server could not be found, the document could not be found on the host server, or the document did not contain information.)

[13]That the full *NTS* reports are not yet available on the BTS web site is surprising, given that the site provides the complete text of statistical reports from other modal administrations (e.g., *1995 Highway Statistics* from the Federal Highway Administration). Recently, the *1996 Transportation Statistics Annual Report* was made directly accessible through the BTS web site, as were the tables in the *1997 NTS*.

Subject Listing

Please check News & Updates to see a listing of products as they become available online.

Safety

❏ Directory of Transportation Data Sources 1996 - You can now add or adjust a Data Source for inclusion in the 1997 edition.
❏ National Transportation Statistics (NTS) 1993
❏ National Transportation Statistics (NTS) 1997 - NTS Tables available for download in MS Excel 5.0 format.
❏ State and Metropolitan Analysis for Regional Transportation (SMART) - Available through the National Transportation Library on the BTS Homepage.
❏ Traffic Safety Data: FARS and GES
❏ Transportation Data Sampler-3
❏ Transportation in the United States: A Review
❏ Transportation Safety
❏ Transportation Statistics Annual Report (TSAR) 1994
❏ Transportation Statistics Annual Report (TSAR) 1995
❏ Transportation Statistics Annual Report (TSAR) 1996 - Available in PDF format.
❏ Transportation Statistics: In Brief

[Alphabetical Listing]   [Media Listing]   [Mode Listing]

[BTS Products Page] [BTS Services] [Order Form]

Feedback? Questions? comments@bts.gov

FIGURE 3-1   Portion of subject index for "Products" section of BTS web site.

up some but not all of the entries under "safety" in the "Products" subject index together with new entries. The entries are annotated; however, the annotations in many instances are not informative about the content of the item listed (e.g., see the listing for "homepage.rtf" in Figure 3-2).

The "Databases" section of the site brings up the National Transportation Data Archive, which contains statistical reports, data sets, and descriptions of data sets, including entries from the Federal Aviation Administration, Federal

Grouped by ● Confidence ○ Subject

excite for web servers found documents about: **safety data** | New Search |

excite for web servers found documents about: **safety data**

❏ 68% **about.htm**

Summary: Welcome to the Office of System Safety's Homepage. Who Are We?

❏ 68% **index.html**

Summary: Fatal Accident Reporting System Database. The Traffic Safety Data set was developed by the Bureau of Transportation Statistics and the National Highway Traffic Safety Administration's (NHTSA) National Center for Statistics and Analysis (NCSA) to make traffic safety data easily accessible and widely available.

❏ 68% **BTS Products - Traffic Safety Data: 1988-1993**

Summary: What is it? The Traffic Safety Data: 1988-1993 was produced by the Bureau of Transportation Statistics to make traffic safety data easily accessible and widely available.

❏ 66% **SMART-SAFETY@BTS.GOVdocFrame.html**

Summary: *NEW* Emergency Medical Services (EMS) Public Information, Education and Relations (PIER) - National Standard Curriculum (PDF file). *NEW* Public Education Video Clips [Served by Federal Railway Administration].

❏ 66% **SMART-SURVEY@BTS.GOVdocFrame.html**

Summary: *NEW* Sample Transportation Surveys. *NEW* Survey of Motor Carriers in the Rochester Transportation Management Area.

❏ 64% **BTS Products - Traffic Safety**

Summary: What is it? The Traffic Safety CD-ROM contains 2 years of statistics from the National Highway Traffic Safety Administration's (NHTSA) Fatal Accident Reporting System (FARS), 1975-1994 and 7 years of statistics from the General Estimates System (GES), 1988-1994 in ASCII format along with its associated technical documentation.

❏ 64% **homepage.rtf**
Summary:{/rtf1/ansi/deff4/deflang1033{/fonttbl{/f4/froman/fcharset0/fprq2TimesNewRoman;}
}   {/colortbl;/red0/green0/blue0;/red0/green0/blue255;/red0/green255/blue255;/red0/

FIGURE 3-2   Results of searching BTS web site for "Safety Data."

green255/blue0;/red255/green0/blue255;/red255/green0/blue0;/red255/green255/blue0;/
red255/green255/blue255;/red0/green0/blue128;/red0/green128/blue128;/red0/green128/
blue0;/red128/green0/blue128;/red128/green0/blue/snext0Normal;} {/*/cs10 /additive Default
ParagraphFont;} } {/info{/title About the Aviation Safety Office} {/author FeliceBrunner} {/
operatorFeliceBrunner}
{/creatim/yr1996/mo3/dy27/hr14/min41} {/revtim/yr1996/mo3/dy28/hr11/min12} {/printim/
yr1996/mo3/dy28/hr11/min29} {/version5} {/edmins131} {/nofpages0} {/nofwords0} {/
nofchars0} {/vern49213} } /widowctrl/ftnbj/aenddoc/noextraspr/prcolbl//fet0/sectd/linex0/
endnhere{/*/pnseclvl1/pnucrm/pnstart1/pnindent720/pnhang{/pntxta.} } {/*/pnseclvl2/pnucltr/
pnstart1/pnind

❑ 64% **ts91395k.html**

Summary: "Drive Smart" Nights at Central Pennsylvania Speedways PENNSYLVANIA PROBLEM IDENTIFICATION Observation of those who frequent professional auto racing events shows that racing fans are more likely than other motorists to drive faster than the speed limit and drive after drinking and are less likely to wear a safety belt. In an effort to communicate directly with this high-risk segment of the driving public, Pennsylvania's Center for Highway Safety Program collaborated with the South Central Pennsylvania Highway Safety Program to establish special safe driving promotions at local speedways throughout 13 counties in Central Pennsylvania.

❑ 64% **ts91395h.html**

Summary: 100% Platinum Pacesetter Safety Belt Honor Roll MARYLAND PROBLEM IDENTIFICATION During the past several years, Maryland law enforcement agencies received extensive state and national recognition for their promotion of safety belt use. Prior goals and programs established by concerned highway safety groups in Maryland helped move communities towards increased safety belt use rates.

❑ 64% **SMART-PUBLIC@BTS.GOVdocFrame.html**

Summary: *NEW* Public Involvement Procedures for New Hampshire Transportation Improvement Projects. 1992 Transportation & Air Quality Planning Guidelines.

❑ 64% **ts91395i.html**

Summary: Cornhusker Highway Community/Corridor Traffic Safety Project NEBRASKA PROBLEM IDENTIFICATION Highway 6, also known as Cornhusker Highway, in Lincoln, Nebraska has a high rate of traffic crashes. The road is a high speed arterial with an average daily traffic flow of 32,000 vehicles and a multitude of access points.

❑ 64% **The National Transportation Safety Section**

Summary: Safety. Take part in our new Communications Center!

❑ 64% **Finding the DOT Records You Want**

Summary: Guide To Finding The DOT Records You Want.

FIGURE 3-2 Continued

FOCUSING ON DATA QUALITY 57

❑ 64% **BTS Products - Transportation Statistics: In Brief**

Summary: Transportation Statistics: In Brief. Transportation Statistics: In Brief is a pocket pamphlet designed to highlight two years of transportation data, 1980 and 1994.

❑ 62% **Major Customers**

Summary: Major Customers. The Office of Airline Information provides the airline financial, traffic and economic data systems that are the critical foundation of DOT's regulatory, advocacy and policy decision-making processes.

❑ 62% **ts91395g.html**

Summary: Accident Location Analysis System IOWA PROBLEM IDENTIFICATION The Bureau of Transportation Safety at the Iowa Department of Transportation (IDOT) maintains a database of traffic records sent in by investigating officers as well as drivers involved in crashes occurring on public road systems in Iowa. All crashes that result in a fatality, a personal injury or at least $500 property damage are included in the database.

❑ 62% **tab9-2.txt**

Summary: TABLE 9.2 AIRLINES (Air Carriers Operating under 14 CFR 121) Accidents, Fatalities, and Rates (Preliminary Data) 1993 Scheduled Nonscheduled Accidents Total 23 0 Fatal 1 0 Fatalities 1 0 Aircraft Hours Flown (000) 1 11,900 624 Departures (000) 1 7,732 312 Accident Rate Per 100,000 Hours Flown Total 0.19 0.00 Fatal 0.01 0.00 Accident Rate Per 100,000 Departures Total 0.30 0.00 Fatal 0.01 0.00 1 Exposure data estimate source: Research and Special Programs Administration and FAA Source: National Transportation Safety ...

❑ 62% **tab9-2.txt**

Summary: TABLE 9.2 AIRLINES (Air Carriers Operating under 14 CFR 121) Accidents, Fatalities, and Rates (Preliminary Data) 1993 Scheduled Nonscheduled Accidents Total 23 0 Fatal 1 0 Fatalities 1 0 Aircraft Hours Flown (000) 1 11,900 624 Departures (000) 1 7,732 312 Accident Rate Per 100,000 Hours Flown Total 0.19 0.00 Fatal 0.01 0.00 Accident Rate Per 100,000 Departures Total 0.30 0.00 Fatal 0.01 0.00 1 Exposure data estimate source: Research and Special Programs Administration and FAA Source: National Transportation Safety ...

❑ 62% **tab9-3.txt**

Summary: TABLE 9.3 AIRLINES (Air Carriers Operating under 14 CFR 121) Fatal Accidents, Fatalities (Preliminary Data) 1993 Location Operator Date Serv. Aircraft Fatalities Total Reported Type On- Type of Total Pass- Crew Others board Accident engers SCHEDULED SERVICE Chicago, IL Simmons 4/4 Psgr ATR 1 0 0 1 48 Ground Airlines 42-300 crewmember dba: struck American by Eagle propeller NONSCHEDULED SERVICE None Source: National Transportation Safety ...

FIGURE 3-2   Continued

❏ 62% **tab9-3.txt**

Summary: TABLE 9.3 AIRLINES (Air Carriers Operating under 14 CFR 121) Fatal Accidents, Fatalities (Preliminary Data) 1993 Location Operator Date Serv. Aircraft Fatalities Total Reported Type On- Type of Total Pass- Crew Others board Accident engers SCHEDULED SERVICE Chicago, IL Simmons 4/4 Psgr ATR 1 0 0 1 48 Ground Airlines 42-300 crewmember dba: struck American by Eagle propeller NONSCHEDULED SERVICE None Source: National Transportation Safety ...

[Results by Excite]

FIGURE 3-2   Continued

Highway Administration, National Highway Traffic Safety Administration, and the Federal Transit Administration, as well as BTS. At present, the archive contains 11 listings, of which some are descriptions of data products rather than data (see Figure 3-3).

To help the user locate additional data and information, the BTS site provides links to the web sites of the other USDOT modal administrations (these links are to the main administrations and not to their statistical units). The BTS site also has links to many other organizations (commercial, private, government, nonprofit, libraries) with some relation to transportation. The user can search any and all of these sites for data; however, their design does not always facilitate such a search. The BTS site itself provides no guidance for users in their search of other sites. Such guidance could take the form of putting the *Directory of Transportation Data Sources* on the BTS site, making its contents searchable by keyword, and, when applicable, adding links to other web sites to obtain more information or to see the actual data. Alternatively, such guidance could be provided through short essays that inform the user of major data series in particular cross-modal topic areas and where to find them.

Data documentation   The BTS web site gives no evidence of the application of consistent standards for the information provided about the quality and limitations of available data. The brief descriptions that are provided in the "Products" section for BTS CD-ROM products vary in content and usefulness (see Appendix E). Each data set listed in the National Transportation Data Archive (see Figure 3-3) has a contents page that links to the following headings: Detailed Description, Reports and Products, Searchable Database (operational as yet for only some of the data sets), Questions and Comments, Methods and Limitations, Future Plans, Applications, and Related Topics. This selection of headings appears potentially very useful; however, to date, there is limited or no information provided for such key headings as Methods and Limitations for many of the data sets in the National Data Archive. Several of the data sets in the archive reproduce publica-

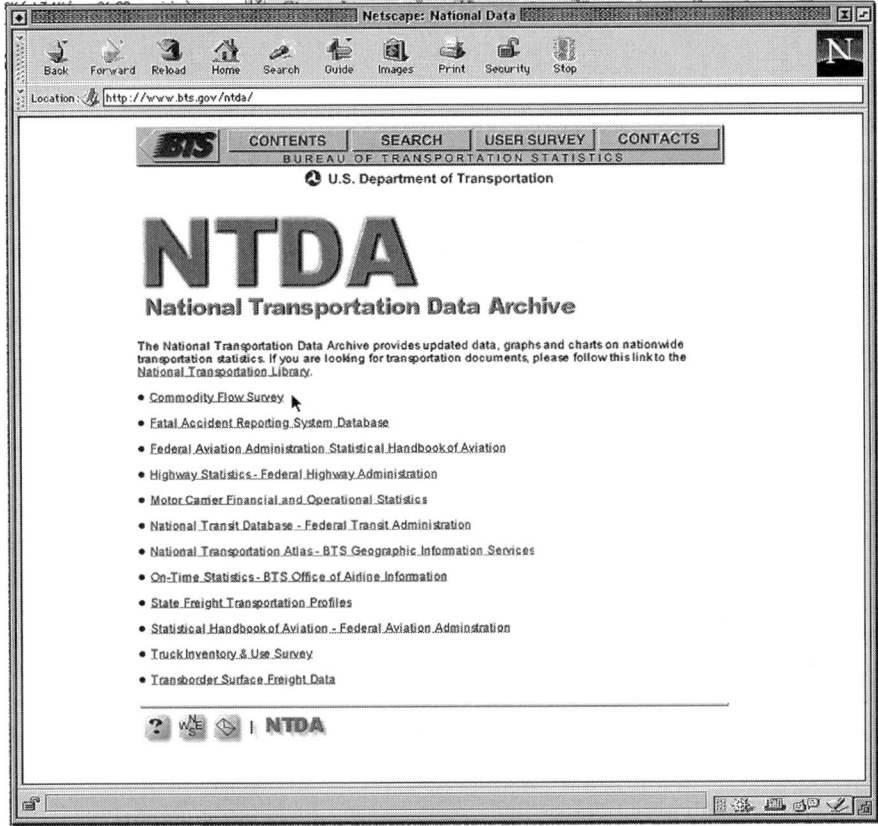

FIGURE 3-3 Contents of National Transportation Data Archive in "Databases" section of BTS web site.

tions from other USDOT modal administrations (e.g., highway statistics); the documentation that is provided in these publications about data collection methods and data quality varies according to the practices of the originating agencies.

At this stage of its development, it may not be feasible for BTS to standardize the documentation for all of the data sets it makes accessible on its web site from the other modal administrations (or other sources), although such standardization should be a goal of the work to develop department-wide quality standards. However, BTS can and should move quickly to standardize documentation for its own data sets and also to standardize and improve the descriptions of its CD-ROM and other products. It should also include on the site a prominent statement to advise users about the importance of understanding the meaning and limitations of available data sets before attempting to work with them. Providing contact names whenever possible for users to learn not only about the content and scope of a data set, but also about its uses and limitations, would be helpful.

DATA EVALUATION AND IMPROVEMENT

Documentation of data quality and relevance is essential for users; however, such documentation is necessarily limited to the extent that a data set has not been evaluated on a range of dimensions. Major responsibilities of statistical agencies are to evaluate their data and, on the basis of such evaluations, to inform users of current limitations of the data and to develop ongoing programs to improve data quality (see National Research Council, 1992b, and Appendix C). To support continuing data improvement, agencies need to conduct statistical research on data collection, processing, and estimation methods and also substantive research on the issues for which the data are compiled (see discussion in Chapter 4). BTS should plan and begin to implement systematic programs of evaluation and improvement of key transportation data sets.

BTS Surveys

As a first priority, BTS should review the evaluations it has completed or has under way for the two major intermodal surveys that it sponsors to determine what further evaluations are needed and what the evaluation results imply for appropriate use of the data and for future design decisions. These two surveys—the Commodity Flow Survey and the American Travel Survey—are the largest component of the BTS budget, accounting for over one-third of BTS expenditures over fiscal years 1994 to 1997, most of which represents funds transferred to the Census Bureau for data collection and processing.

Some evaluations that the Census Bureau, working with BTS, has completed of the 1995 ATS include assessments of "recall bias" and "time-in-sample bias."[14] Recall bias is inferred when respondents report a behavior more frequently for a period closer to the interview than for a period that is farther away in time. Time-in-sample bias is inferred when respondents change their behavior or reporting of their behavior over successive interviews. Both types of bias are important to evaluate for the ATS because it consisted of four interviews with the same households, each interview covering a 3-month reporting period.

Additional types of evaluation studies that would be important to undertake for both the ATS and CFS include comparisons of the characteristics of survey respondents with nonrespondents (including the implications of differences for the accuracy of key survey estimates) and comparisons of selected survey esti-

---

[14]Two of the BTS staff are sworn census agents, so that they can work with confidential microdata at the Census Bureau for evaluation purposes.

mates with estimates from other data sources. For example, trip reporting behavior could be compared for the 1995 ATS with the 1995 NPTS and the 1995 Consumer Expenditure Survey (CEX). Aggregate comparisons between two data systems must be made with care to allow for differences in definitions and data collection and processing procedures, but the identification of discrepancies can lead to further research to determine reasons and suggest ways to improve one or both data systems.

A comparative evaluation study that could be particularly useful for the ATS concerns transportation costs. Because of a belief that households are poor reporters of costs, the ATS questionnaire does not ask about trip costs. BTS expects that the U.S. Travel Data Center, a private organization, will develop model-based estimates of long-distance trip costs on the basis of trip characteristics. When such estimates are developed, it would be useful to compare them with trip cost information from the CEX.

For subsequent rounds of the CFS and the ATS, BTS should consider additional research and evaluation both prior to and as part of the surveys. For example, cognitive research techniques could be used to evaluate and improve the ATS questionnaire. Given the importance of information on travel costs, it could be worthwhile to embed an experiment within the ATS in which trip costs are obtained from a subsample of respondents and the completeness of their reporting is evaluated against other sources.

The results of evaluation studies should be used, together with assessments of the usefulness of CFS and ATS data by BTS staff and other analysts, to guide periodic reevaluations of the overall design of the two surveys. At present, the plans for the two surveys are to continue the historical pattern of conducting them at 5-year intervals with large sample sizes. (The 1995 ATS sample includes 80,000 households, the largest sample size of any U.S. national household survey.) The large sample sizes in the 5-year design are intended to support needed subnational geographic analysis of interarea travel flows, but the cost is that updates are available only at relatively long intervals.

An alternative design for the two surveys would be to have continuing small samples that provide national estimates on, say, an annual basis and to augment those samples periodically to obtain more detailed interarea data. Yet another design would be to have small national samples with added samples each year for specific areas that would "roll" across the country in some fashion. The rolling sample design would be helpful in the congressional budget process, in that it would smooth out peaks and valleys in required funding levels. However, the subnational estimates it provides could be difficult to interpret because the information for each year's area sample would necessarily pertain to transportation by residents or shippers within the specified areas and not also to movements of people or goods into those areas from nonsample areas.

Careful consideration of transportation analysis needs and of the costs of alternative designs will be required to determine an optimal strategy for how often the surveys are fielded and the corresponding sample sizes and designs. That strategy may turn out to be the current design of large surveys at 5-year intervals; however, that design should be chosen on the basis of research, evaluation, and user input and not just continued from the past. (Evaluation results should also inform other design choices, such as length of recall period and questionnaire content and wording.)[15] Finally, an assessment of the design of the ATS, and perhaps of the CFS as well, should take into account other similar surveys and the possibilities for coordinating or integrating their designs (see Appendix F).

Other Data

Once BTS gains experience and expertise in evaluating its own data systems and a reputation for excellence in this regard, then it will be in a position to advise other USDOT statistical units about evaluation and improvement of their data systems, particularly from the perspective of improving the usefulness of the data for cross-modal, system-wide analyses of transportation issues. Such a role is in keeping with the establishment of BTS in the 1991 ISTEA as the statistical agency with a broad mandate to improve transportation data within the department.

BTS can begin immediately to work with the other USDOT modal administrations to identify additional information on data quality and limitations that should be added to the descriptions on the BTS web site and in BTS compendia and reference publications. (This work will naturally be part of BTS's strengthened mandate to develop data quality standards for USDOT.) Cooperative efforts with other modal administrations to undertake more extensive documentation and to refine existing evaluation and improvement programs (or to launch new programs) for their data systems will require a carefully planned and staged approach. Work toward that end should be guided by a vision of transportation data needs within which to identify priority areas for attention in the short, medium, and long term (see Chapter 4) and by the data quality standards that are developed by BTS in cooperation with the other modal administrations.

RECOMMENDATIONS

Staffing

(2) BTS should be authorized to appoint an associate director for statis-

---

[15]Another design choice is whether to include a longitudinal component, in which data are obtained from the same reporting units over time, as was done to a limited extent in the 1995 ATS (households were interviewed four times over 1 year). Longitudinal data permit analysis of complex behavior patterns but can require significant resources and pose such problems as attrition (sample units dropping out of the survey) and time-in-sample bias.

tical methods and research at the Senior Executive Service level to provide leadership in improving the quality of transportation statistics. BTS should give priority to hiring highly qualified staff with expertise in statistical methods.

Quality Standards

(3) In the reauthorization of BTS, the Congress should strengthen current law by assigning responsibility to BTS to establish data quality standards, consistent with good statistical practice, that are binding throughout USDOT and available for use by transportation agencies outside USDOT and for reference by the public. The reauthorization should also:

- require the secretary of transportation to appoint a departmental standards committee, chaired by the BTS director and with representatives from the USDOT statistical units, to work with BTS in developing department-wide data quality standards and
- require BTS to prepare every 2 years a report to the Congress that identifies improvements achieved in data quality by BTS and the statistical units in the other USDOT modal administrations and in the provision of information about quality to data users.

Data Documentation

(4) BTS should improve the documentation of the transportation data it makes available so that users can readily assess their quality, including accuracy, variability, and comparability across transportation modes and over time.

4

Ensuring Relevance

A statistical agency must not only document, evaluate, and improve the quality of the data within its subject area, but it must also ensure that there are relevant data on topics of importance to policy makers, planners, and researchers in the field. The previous chapter addressed the immediate necessity for the Bureau of Transportation Statistics (BTS) to focus on data quality and to build a strong statistical staff to carry out its responsibilities for quality improvement. This chapter addresses areas that BTS should undertake to improve the relevance of transportation data to meet important user needs.

The 1991 Intermodal Surface Transportation Efficiency Act (ISTEA) assigns several functions to BTS that have the goal of ensuring the relevance of transportation data for policy making and other purposes. They include: developing appropriate indicators for the transportation system; coordinating the collection of transportation data by USDOT with other federal agencies and collecting data to fill gaps; and identifying unmet information needs and ways to meet those needs. These functions are commonly undertaken by statistical agencies, but to date BTS has done relatively little on them. Work needs to begin.

Central to a statistical agency's ability to improve data relevance, and more generally to determine priorities for its work, is that it have a broad vision of a comprehensive data system that can serve the information needs of users over the medium and long term. In this chapter, after first defining what we mean by "relevance," we discuss the development by BTS of a vision of a comprehensive transportation data system and how that vision and other considerations should factor into its development of a long-range plan for implementing all aspects of its mandate.

We then discuss priority areas for BTS to undertake to improve the relevance of transportation data for policy making and other uses. They include: the development of key national transportation indicators; an increased role in coordinating the collection of transportation data, in particular, the compilation of an annual statistical budget as a data coordination mechanism for USDOT; the establishment of regular mechanisms for identifying user information needs, in particular, effective two-way communication channels with states and metropolitan planning organizations, building on the work that BTS has under way in this area; and the assessment and further development of BTS's analysis programs and publications. Primary recommendations appear at the end of the chapter.

DIMENSIONS OF RELEVANCE

"Relevance" concerns substantive aspects of data systems that affect their usefulness. Dimensions of relevance include the following:

- *The appropriateness of concepts*, which means that the concepts a data system is intended to measure are those that can help policy makers and analysts understand trends and behaviors of concern to them and the implications of program and policy changes. Conceptual appropriateness must be reviewed in light of changing conditions. For example, with concern about the effects of economic growth on the environment and nonrenewable resources, there is growing interest in concepts of national income and gross national product that account for natural resource depletion, pollution, and other environmental costs. More narrowly, beginning in December 1991, the Bureau of Economic Analysis has featured gross domestic product (GDP), and not gross national product (GNP), as the more appropriate concept by which to measure U.S. output for comparative analysis with other countries in today's global economy.[1]

- *The match between concepts, operational definitions, and measurements*, which implies that the theoretical concepts of importance to data users are operationalized by appropriately defined empirical variables that, in turn, are accurately and reliably measured (see Bonnen, 1977:395-396). Many concepts are difficult to operationalize. For example, the economic cost of transportation fatalities and injuries is an important concept for which to have data, but it may be difficult to operationalize such a concept with an appropriate proxy variable or combination of variables that can be measured empirically. For example, should the costs include the immediate costs of medical treatment, emergency system use, vehicle repair, etc.? The long-term costs over the lifetime of accident victims of health care, public assistance, lost productivity, foregone tax revenues, etc.? Estimates of the value of lost quality of life? The choice of operational definition affects the relevance of the concept for policy and research use and also

---

[1] GDP includes the output produced by labor and property located in the United States, including the output of U.S.-located establishments of foreign-owned enterprises; GNP includes the output attributable to labor and property supplied by U.S. residents (see Bureau of the Census, 1996b:439-440).

the ability to obtain accurate measurements. In the example, the broader the operationalization of the concept, the more difficult the measurement process.

- *More generally, the appropriate level of detail* in a data system in terms of the specificity and range of subject matter and geographic detail that it provides to inform current and emerging policy and research interests. Appropriateness of detail must be reviewed continually in light of changing conditions and policy concerns. As examples, more data are needed for the fast-growing services sector of the economy to support public- and private-sector policy making and planning than was true in the past, and more data are needed on intermodal transport to address increasingly important transportation policy concerns.
- *Timeliness of statistical information*, which denotes the length of time between the occurrence of some event or the act of measuring some attribute of interest and the availability of statistics to the user. For example, the Bureau of Labor Statistics provides a monthly update of the labor market status of the economy. Wise decisions on the periodicity of data collection are a function of the rate of change and causes of change in estimates as well as the nature of decisions taken on the basis of the estimates.

The implications of a statistical agency's focusing on data relevance in terms of appropriateness of concepts and their measurement, level of subject matter and geographic detail, and timeliness are that it must identify needs for data among current users, gaps in available data systems, and possibilities for the agency to inform the policy debates of the future. This process, combined with a comprehensive understanding of the field, permits the agency to define sets of indicators that offer great relevance to current and future users and to provide other kinds of useful data.

In its efforts to ensure relevance, it is important that a statistical agency seek ways to contain the costs and burden of data collection, processing, and analysis by keeping abreast of new methods and technologies that have the potential for cost savings and by looking for ways to cut back on less important data (e.g, through reductions in sample size or frequency). There will always be more data demands than can be satisfied, particularly in an era of increasingly constrained budgets, and it is critical for a statistical agency to evaluate data needs to determine priority areas for new and improved data and also areas for which reductions are possible.

A VISION OF A COMPREHENSIVE TRANSPORTATION DATA SYSTEM

Key to BTS's ability to ensure the relevance of transportation data and to make wise choices among competing activities to improve both data relevance and quality is that it have a broad vision of transportation data (see recommendation 5 at the end of the chapter). The vision should encompass the information needs of transportation policy makers, planners, and researchers in the medium and long term and the characteristics of a comprehensive data system that could best serve those needs. BTS will not necessarily or even likely itself develop all of the data that are required to implement the vision. Much of the specific work to be undertaken will be done outside BTS: by other USDOT modal administrations, by other parts of the federal statistical system, and by states, localities, and private organizations. However, if BTS is to fill the leadership role set out for it by the 1991 ISTEA, then it must have an overarching vision of the data requirements in key constituencies in the transportation field.

How can BTS, as a priority effort, go about constructing such a vision and refreshing it periodically? One way is to ask relevant constituencies such questions as the following:

What are seen as important national policy concerns in transportation, how are they changing, and what are the implications for data? The 1991 ISTEA called for a reorientation of transportation planning to address intermodal and multimodal issues and concerns. The reauthorization of ISTEA is likely to continue a cross-modal planning focus and may single out other important policy issues for the transportation community as well. The continuing public concern with such issues as the safety of the transportation system, the quality of the environment, and the costs and availability of energy sources will also have important implications for transportation planning and investment. In developing a vision of information needs and a data system to address them, BTS must assess the data requirements of continuing and emerging national transportation policy concerns as seen by the Congress, the administration, and others, including states, metropolitan planning organizations, industry, and the general public.

What changes are occurring in the economy and society that suggest the need for new data or the reassignment of priorities among areas? The nature and pace of future social and economic change are hard to foresee with any great precision; however, broad trends are identifiable that are likely to have implications for a comprehensive transportation data system that can serve user needs. Such trends include the aging of the population; the continued suburbanization of people and industry; growing pressures on the environment; the computerization of homes, schools, and businesses; and the globalization of the economy and continued growth in international trade. BTS could elaborate scenarios in these and other areas and consider the possible data implications for transportation. While not making too much of the results of such scenario-building, BTS could identify areas in which modest additional data collection, or somewhat different data collection, could help the transportation community anticipate and respond to important societal trends.

As an example, rapid growth over the next few decades in the proportion of employed people who telecommute to work via computer, telephone, and fax at home can be expected to change the kinds of infrastructure investments that are required for an efficient transportation system, compared with a continuation of current work practices. If the projected differences in the kinds of needed investment are significant, then it could be important to the transportation community to have data with which to assess more accurately the likely rates of change in home-based employment linked with data on residence patterns. Such data inputs could include not only survey questions about current workplaces, but also survey questions about the likelihood that respondents will work part or all of their hours at home in the next year, or next 5 years, and what factors might cause them to make such a change.

What topics and information needs are still relevant from the past? In addition to new and modified data to respond to emerging concerns, there is always a need for continuing time series to support trend analysis and provide benchmarks against which to measure change. The question is which series are critically important to continue and which could be reduced in scope, frequency, or sample size or redesigned in other ways (e.g., by converting an administrative records system to sample-based reporting or using new collection technology) in order to free up resources for other areas or to reduce the overall costs and burden of transportation data collection.

In the transportation area, data on safety are clearly an important continuing need, particularly for USDOT, given the extensive involvement of the federal government in safety issues and safety regulation in all modes of transportation. There are likely to be other such areas as well. However, there are also likely to be areas in which the data that are currently collected are of less value to continue in the future (e.g., because of lesser policy concern) or that could be collected just as effectively by other organizations or other means. For example, detailed information on financial and operating characteristics of some kinds of common carriers might be one such area. Decisions to reduce or eliminate long-established data series are always difficult to make. However, a statistical agency that is striving to improve data relevance must have a vision of a comprehensive data system that is dynamic and allows for the retirement of obsolescent data series along with the emergence of new and modified series.

A BTS IMPLEMENTATION PLAN

A critically important task for BTS to undertake in the near future is the development of a long-term strategy for implementing its mission to improve both the relevance and quality of transportation data. BTS's mandate encompasses a large, almost daunting, array of functions and responsibilities. A structured implementation plan that specifies short-term, intermediate, and long-term goals in each of BTS's main programmatic areas is a necessity in order for BTS to work toward its vision of a comprehensive transportation data system and evolve as a statistical agency for USDOT. Without such a plan, BTS's energies are likely to be dissipated in striving to do more than it reasonably can. Also, without such a plan, the inevitable pressures from continuing areas of responsibility (e.g., for data dissemination) may result in continued deferment of needed initiatives in other areas (e.g., development of quality standards). BTS must have a roadmap with a well-blocked-out route to guide its activities, help it develop the necessary staff capabilities, and build a reputation as an effective agency that, over time, is fulfilling its mandate from the ISTEA.

The implementation plan should identify overall priorities among BTS's major functions for the short and longer term and, within each functional area, identify specific activities, goals, and timetables.[2] BTS's vision of a comprehensive transportation data system should provide the context for the development of the implementation plan. For example, such a vision should help determine a priority sequence for the development of national transportation indicators. Another source of input to the plan is this report, which identifies broad areas of high priority, including work to develop department-wide quality standards, increased emphasis on documenting and evaluating data quality, and work to develop national indicators, at the same time recommending decreased emphasis on the quantity of data disseminated. Still other sources of input, for both general and specific priorities and goals, include the constituencies or customers for transportation data—national policy makers, state and local agencies, private-sector organizations, and academic researchers.

The development of a vision of a comprehensive transportation data system and the development of a long-term strategy for implementing BTS's mandate are difficult, time-consuming tasks that represent added responsibilities for BTS staff. As would be true for any attempt at a serious long-range planning process, it is likely that BTS's initial efforts will produce areas for which it is not clear how to proceed or for which there is less complete articulation of ideas and goals than for other areas. Also, there must be flexibility to revise and further develop the vision and plan as circumstances change and new knowledge and experience are gained. Nonetheless, it is critical that BTS make its best attempt to envision the future requirements for transportation data and to plan its own future so that, for the long term, it has an overall sense of direction and, for the short and medium term, it has a set of goals that are feasible, contribute to the long-term agenda, and make it possible for the agency to demonstrate a solid record of accomplishment over time.

ENSURING RELEVANCE: TRANSPORTATION INDICATORS

The 1991 ISTEA mandates BTS to establish and implement, in cooperation with the modal administrations, the states, and other federal officials, a compre-

---

[2] BTS recently outlined its goals in specific areas for fiscal 1997 and 1998 (provided in a background document for the Advisory Council on Transportation Statistics). These goals should be reexamined as part of a longer-range planning process.

hensive, long-term program for collection and analysis of data relating to the performance of the national transportation system. The Transportation Research Board report, *Data for Decisions* (National Research Council, 1992a), urged, as a high priority, that a new transportation data center, which is now BTS, develop a national transportation performance monitoring system. It developed a list of important attributes of the transportation system, for which it suggested one or more types of indicators (this list is reproduced in Table 4-1).

We agree that a high priority for BTS is to develop a consistent, easily understood, and useful set of indicators of key aspects of the transportation system (see recommendation 6 at the end of the chapter). Most statistical agencies produce indicators (usually regular time series) in their areas: examples are monthly and quarterly gross domestic product (GDP) estimates produced by the Bureau of Economic Analysis; monthly Consumer Price Index (CPI) and unemployment rate estimates produced by the Bureau of Labor Statistics; monthly retail sales, monthly housing starts, and annual poverty statistics produced by the Census Bureau; annual high school and college completion and dropout rates and periodic assessments of levels of student achievement produced by the National Center for Education Statistics; and annual vital statistics, which include estimates of births and deaths and mortality rates by cause, produced by the National Center for Health Statistics. Each of these indicator series is important in informing the public and contributing to the policy debate in its area; some of them have significant effects on the economy and public- and private-sector decision making. In other words, appropriately developed indicators provide highly relevant data for policy making and general public awareness.

It is a heavy responsibility to produce such important statistics. There are often difficult conceptual, definitional, and measurement issues involved in developing a single reliable and credible indicator to represent a complicated socioeconomic phenomenon or construct (e.g., GDP, unemployment, poverty); even two or three indicators may not be adequate. Moreover, the policy use of key indicators can bring unwelcome publicity to a statistical agency, which may be hard pressed to explain the proper interpretation of its statistics and to defend the concepts and methods against politically motivated criticism and misuse.

Furthermore, the development of indicators should not be the only focus of a statistical agency in terms of providing relevant data. Thus, indicators cannot serve such important needs as that of researchers for rich, multivariate data sets (e.g., longitudinal surveys) with which to analyze complex trends and behaviors. Nonetheless, key statistical indicators are important for both the public and policy makers, and statistical agencies can gain stature and support from the responsibility to produce them. Also, such responsibility can help an agency set priorities for improvement of key concepts, definitions, and data sources that are needed to support the development of indicators and to support more in-depth analysis as well.

Indicators, Not Performance Measures

In discussing BTS's role in developing transportation indicators, we explicitly use the term "statistical indicator" instead of "performance measure" or a similar term. The latter has a judgmental or regulatory connotation that is inappropriate for a statistical agency.

Indeed, there has been considerable concern among the states about the recent interest on the part of the federal government in assessing the performance of the transportation system. The states are wary of jurisdiction-specific performance measures that might be used for such purposes as allocating federal transportation funds, particularly in light of the difficulties of developing valid measures that appropriately take account of measurement problems and varying conditions at state and local levels. (As examples, measures of road conditions should adjust for such factors as types and extent of usage, and measures of highway traffic congestion should adjust for such factors as population density and the availability of public transit.)

Such concerns are not limited to transportation. For many years, the states largely opposed the development of comparable cross-jurisdiction indicators of children's educational progress. A major survey, the National Assessment of Educational Progress (NAEP), was originally designed so that only national-level and not also state-level estimates could be produced from the data. However, increasing public concern about educational issues has led to a willingness on the part of the states to compare their performance, and the NAEP was recently redesigned to provide state-level estimates.

What all this means is that a statistical agency must approach the development of indicators with care. To the extent that meaningful national-level indicators can be developed, they should be an important focus of the agency.

BTS has already established as a priority goal for fiscal 1998 to begin work on transportation indicators. BTS proposes a cooperative activity with the other USDOT modal administrations, such as the Federal Aviation Administration and the Federal Highway Administration, in which they would first identify appropriate topics and concepts for indicators and BTS would then provide technical advice on implementation. A motivation for the development of indicators is the 1993 Government Performance and Results Act, which requires federal agencies to establish performance measures of their output.

We urge BTS to move forward with its plans to help the other modal administrations identify performance indicators for their own programs. In general, as BTS builds its statistical staff and capabilities, it should be able increasingly to be helpful to the other modal administrations not only in the development of indicators and other kinds of statistical data, but also in advising on ways to improve the cost-effectiveness and usefulness of the large amounts of data that many of them collect for purposes of program administration and regulation.

At the same time, we urge BTS to develop a small set of key national statis-

TABLE 4-1 Transportation System Indicators Suggested in *Data for Decisions*

Data Attribute and Descriptor	Indicators
Supply	
System	
General characteristics	Inventory information (e.g., miles of system)
Coverage	Unit of system per land area or population
Physical condition	Index of condition (e.g., pavement serviceability rating)
	Age of facilities
	Maintenance expenditures per unit of system
Capacity	Vehicles/persons per hour, tons per hour
Fare or fee structure	Range of prices, prices per passenger-mile/ton-mile, price/service options
Elasticity of supply	Percentage change in supply relative to a 1 percent change in cost
Providers	
General characteristics	Number and size of public providers/common carriers/private carriers and providers
Financial condition	Balance sheet and income statement data
Demand	
User characteristics	National demographic and economic data (e.g., age, sex, income, etc.)
Passenger	
Freight	Bulk, density, shipment sizes, containerization, hazardous contents
Activity levels	Traffic counts, volumes, arrivals/departures
Flows	Origin-final destination volumes by trip purpose, distance, mode, passenger and freight characteristics
Elasticity of demand	Percentage change in demand relative to a 1 percent change in price or other measurable attributes of service quality

Performance

Safety and personal security	Total number of accidents, deaths, and injuries, by market
	Number of accidents, deaths, and injuries per mile and per capita, by market
	Percentage of accidents by severity level, by market
	Number and type of security incidents, by service population, by mode
Access	Share of population and households living within defined distances and travel times from airports and for scheduled surface transportation
	Percentage of system facilities and services handicapped accessible
Level	Frequency (e.g., runs per hour/day), average wait time, headways
	Number of transfers per commuter or freight shipment relative to average trip/shipment length
Efficiency	Load factors per unit of capacity available, by market and mode
Quality	Percentage on-time performance, average delay time, by market
	Value of goods damaged in transit
	Value of inventory in transit (average day)
Cost	Cost per trip and unit of travel

Impacts

Economic growth	Average days in inventory held by industry
	Distribution costs as percentage of domestic retail prices/landed export prices
	Tourism receipts, domestic and international trips
National security	Condition and capacity of commercial transportation facilities and special military transport requirements in defense-essential corridors
	Percentage of defense-essential facilities above capacity limits
	Percentage service interruptions and cancellations, by market
Environmental quality/land use	Vehicle emissions levels in nonattainment areas
	Tons of greenhouse gas emissions from transportation sector
	Acres of wetlands affected by construction of transportation facilities
	Number of incidents and extent of spills from transport carriage on waterways
Energy use	Energy use by appropriate energy measure per mile of travel, by market

SOURCE: National Research Council (1992a:Table 2-1).

tical indicators of the transportation system that are relevant to policy and public concerns that it publishes on its own behalf as a statistical agency. (Some indicators—e.g., trends in airline safety—may serve the purposes of both BTS and another modal administration and could be developed and published jointly with the appropriate administration.) BTS's vision of a comprehensive transportation data system should inform its choice of priority areas for indicators, along with input from the other agencies in USDOT and transportation constituencies outside USDOT. Because of BTS's responsibility to improve transportation data for cross-modal, system-wide analyses, the statistical indicators it decides to develop and publish should feature cross-modal concepts and concerns.[3]

What Indicators and in What Form?

The challenge for BTS is to identify important aspects of the national transportation system for which it is possible to develop meaningful and reliable indicators. Transportation is largely local, yet it has national effects. For example, the functioning of the highway, rail, and air systems at a major transportation hub like Chicago affects not only the local economy and well-being, but also the national economy and international trade. The difficulty is to develop indicators that have national meaning when appropriate data may be hard to obtain and to interpret.

The Transportation Research Board report, *Data for Decisions* (National Research Council, 1992a), identified several key areas for which it would be useful to have national indicators but for which data are currently difficult to compare across transportation modes: safety; access to services by such groups as elderly, disabled, low-income, and rural populations; and the efficiency and quality of service provided by the transportation system. BTS has covered some of these topics in its *Transportation Statistics Annual Reports (TSARs)*, as well as other topics. The *1996 TSAR* includes chapters on passenger travel and the movement of freight, with tables on the physical condition of highways, runways and aircraft, and other transportation facilities; the role of transportation in the economy; safety; energy use; and transportation and the environment. Although there is much material in these analyses that could support the development of key indicators, there are also many hurdles to overcome.

In the important area of safety, the *1996 TSAR* notes some of the conceptual and measurement problems for developing meaningful trend indicators. One con-

---

[3] In this regard, *Data for Decisions* (National Research Council, 1992a:32-37) recommends that indicators be developed for types of markets rather than for transportation modes. As an example, cross-modal indicators of travel delays might be developed for intercity markets, such as an indicator that looks specifically at weak links between modes (e.g., highway or rail connections to airports). Such an indicator could help policy makers identify a fuller range of options for improvement of transportation infrastructure than is likely to emerge from analysis of indicators that pertain to particular transportation modes.

ceptual issue is the need to relate trends in injuries and fatalities to measures of risk exposure. The more that people use the transportation system, the more they are exposed to the risk of accidents, so that such measures as fatalities or injuries per number of hours of operation or per unit distance of travel are needed to adjust the raw data appropriately. The appropriate measure of risk exposure may differ across transportation modes, which in turn can make it difficult to compare trends across modes.

The *1996 TSAR* further notes deficiencies and inconsistencies in the reporting of accidents across transportation modes and governmental jurisdictions, particularly for crashes that involve property damage only and for crashes that involve injuries but not fatalities. Information is also inadequate with which to assess the role of environmental conditions (e.g., weather, lighting) and other contributing factors (e.g., human fatigue) in causing accidents.

There is clearly much to be done to develop consistent and useful indicators in transportation safety, as well as other areas. BTS will need to work closely with statistical and analysis units in the other USDOT modal administrations, with states and metropolitan planning organizations, and with the transportation community at large to identify priority areas for indicators and appropriate data and methods for developing useful time series.

As a way to proceed, we suggest that BTS look first to build on a few of the data series that are produced by other USDOT modal administrations and consider how it can add value to them and what new series should be developed to fill existing gaps. BTS should also consider methods to integrate already existing data from BTS, other USDOT modal administrations, and other federal statistical agencies to develop key indicators.

With regard to the form of presenting indicators, we suggest that BTS establish as a goal regular publication—at first annually and moving to a more frequent schedule as feasible and desirable—of a document containing 10 to 20 items that are relevant to policy issues in the transportation field. The publication could be in the form of a freestanding chartbook with back-up statistical information and short analyses of the implications of the material presented. (It could also be a supplement to another publication.)[4]

The focus of the chartbook should reflect key policy concerns, perhaps changing as policy issues do. For example, BTS might plan a few series to explain the effects of increased trade on commodity flow changes, mode of shipment changes, and differences occurring because of changing trade relationships with the North American Free Trade Agreement, the European Community, and the Far East. Similarly, it might plan a series to track the effects on commodity transport of such industry changes as the pending railroad consolidation on the East Coast.

---

[4]Such a chartbook (or supplement) would complement rather than replace the annual *National Transportation Statistics* report; the latter publication brings together for reference purposes many more tables than would appear in a chartbook but without accompanying analyses.

BTS might also consider using data produced by the Bureau of Labor Statistics on employment and combining them with data from the American Travel Survey and the Nationwide Personal Transportation Survey on travel from place of residence to place of work, including the modes used by workers, their costs, and availability. Another set of indicators, as noted previously, might deal with safety—in the air, on the highways, and other modes. Another approach might be to select one of the themes used in the *TSARs* and develop one or more indicators to inform the public about progress—for example, changes in transportation productivity or changes in the relationship between transportation and the environment. (See the section below on "Analysis Programs" for a discussion of how a chartbook of indicators could relate to the *TSARs* and how the latter could usefully be reconfigured.)

COORDINATION OF DATA COLLECTION AND FILLING GAPS

It is important for a statistical agency to coordinate data collection in its area to the extent feasible. Coordination is necessary to make the most cost-effective use of scarce resources to provide relevant, high-quality information for such purposes as developing appropriate statistical indicators and directly serving the information needs of policy makers and other users. (Relatedly, a statistical agency should establish regular sources of input from data users, producers, and methodologists about priority information needs and methods to supply them—see the section below on "Identifying User Needs.") Effective mechanisms for coordination (and input) are required to identify:

- areas of overlap in data collection for which it may be possible and desirable to reduce duplication and associated costs and burdens on respondents and thereby free up resources for other needed data;
- areas for which no data system currently provides relevant measures and for which it may be possible to fill gaps;
- linkages among data systems that may increase their relevance and analytical power; and
- innovations in data collection and analysis methods that may improve the quality of measures across data systems.

There are at least three domains for coordination of data collection in the transportation field: coordination within USDOT; coordination between USDOT and other federal statistical and program agencies; and coordination between USDOT and such key data providers and users as states and metropolitan planning organizations. We recommend that BTS take a major step to facilitate data coordination among the modal administrations in USDOT through a department-wide statistical budget.

A USDOT Statistical Budget

USDOT supports a large number of data collection and analysis programs, with significant statistical activities in almost every modal administration (see Appendix B). To the existing programs, BTS has added new data collection systems on intermodal flows of passengers and freight. We believe it would help USDOT evaluate and improve the relevance and cost-effectiveness of its large array of statistical activities to have BTS prepare each year a consolidated statistical budget for the department (see recommendation 7 at the end of the chapter). BTS could follow the example of the Statistical Policy Division in the U.S. Office of Management and Budget, which brought together information on agencies' proposed fiscal 1998 statistical budgets across the entire federal government for purposes of program review and decision making among competing priorities.[5]

For USDOT, BTS should compile budget information from all of the modal administrations about their statistical programs, including supporting justification. BTS could organize this material in several ways—for example, by subject area as well as by modal administration and agency. It should add commentary as appropriate—for example, noting relationships among programs in different modal administrations or pointing out user needs that no USDOT data collection program currently addresses.

BTS would not determine the budget allocations for any other modal administration. Rather, the consolidated statistical budget would be available for the secretary's use in making final proposed budget allocations to transmit to OMB. It would help clarify for the secretary what the individual modal administrations see as priorities for data collection and analysis. At the same time, it would help the secretary determine how well the agencies' priorities accord with department-wide needs and whether some reallocation of resources among data programs within a modal administration would enable the department to be more cost-effective in providing relevant data for policy purposes and to serve other important needs of the transportation community. To ensure that the preparation of a USDOT statistical budget becomes institutionalized and integrated into the department's decision making, the reauthorization of BTS should directly assign to BTS the responsibility for compiling the statistical budget each year.

We repeat that the USDOT statistical budget would be compiled and annotated by BTS but that BTS would not make budget decisions for any other modal administration. Also, the statistical budget would not include all USDOT data programs. Many data collection systems in USDOT provide modal administra-

---

[5] The Statistical Policy Division some years ago regularly produced cross-cutting statistical budgets as part of the preparation of the president's budget submission to Congress. The practice then lapsed and was just resumed this year. (Routinely, the division produces a cross-cutting description of federal statistical activities after the budget preparation is completed—i.e., to document rather than to inform decision making—see, e.g., Executive Office of the President, 1997b.)

tions with information for program management and regulation and have few statistical uses. Examples are the large number of operational databases of the Federal Aviation Administration (e.g., the Aircraft Registration System and Manufacturing Inspection Management Information System—see National Research Council, 1992a:111-114). The budgets for operating such data systems would not be included in the USDOT statistical budget, except for that portion that may be devoted to statistical analysis of the data for public use.[6]

Practically speaking, the USDOT statistical budget would include the budgets of the major statistical units in the modal administrations (e.g., the Safety Data Services Division in the Federal Aviation Administration—see Appendix B), plus other programs that are not lodged within a separate statistical unit but that the modal administration identifies as having an important statistical component. Indeed, the preparation of the USDOT statistical budget may identify areas in which it would be helpful to a modal administration and for transportation policy analysis, planning, and research more generally to develop the statistical applications of an operational database. As BTS enhances its statistical capabilities and achieves excellence in its own operations, it should be increasingly able to offer technical assistance to the other modal administrations in this regard.

Other Coordination Activities

There are other coordination activities that BTS should consider working into its implementation plan, as available resources and the demands of other priorities permit. For example, BTS could undertake periodic reviews of existing transportation data systems to determine how well they meet the requirements for development of indicators on specific topics and, more generally, how well they contribute to BTS's vision of a comprehensive transportation data system. Such reviews may identify data gaps that are important to fill. They may also identify opportunities for linking or integrating data systems to achieve such goals as making the combined data relevant for a broader range of analyses, improving data quality by such means as standardizing definitions for key variables, and reducing costs.

An obvious first priority for a cross-system data review would be for BTS to look at sources of data on intermodal transportation, including its two flagship intermodal surveys—the Commodity Flow Survey and the American Travel Sur-

---

[6]The Statistical Policy Division in the U.S. Office of Management and Budget faces a similar issue of defining which data programs to include in the cross-cutting federal statistical budget: the criterion used is that *statistical* programs of $500,000 or more in annual expenditures are to be included. As an example, the budget includes the Statistics of Income program in the Internal Revenue Service, which produces statistical publications and data files from tax return data, suitably processed to protect the confidentiality of the information for tax filing units, but the budget does not include the vastly larger costs of the Internal Revenue Service to enter the data from tax returns, calculate taxes owed and refunds due, and monitor compliance.

vey—and other possibly relevant data sources. In Appendix F, we briefly review sources of data on household travel and develop some ideas about data linkage opportunities and remaining data gaps (see also Bureau of Transportation Statistics, 1993c, 1995:96-102).

Conducting cross-system data reviews, as well as carrying out other kinds of coordination activities, will require that BTS involve appropriate agencies through working groups, interagency committees, and the like. In some instances, it will be necessary to involve not only one or more agencies in USDOT, but also outside agencies—for example, other federal statistical and program agencies.

Experience has demonstrated the difficulty of achieving effective interagency collaboration, particularly when the agencies involved are from different departments or levels of government. The history of a short-lived federal interagency transportation statistics coordinating committee that was in existence in the early 1990s illustrates the problem. The committee initially attracted a large attendance to exchange information; however, no action agenda was developed, attendance fell off, and the committee became moribund. This is a common pattern with interagency groups, as participants are pulled back to the agendas of their own agencies and the activities of the interagency group become largely ones of show and tell.

Generally, an effective interagency group requires that agencies be involved because they want to be, believe they can accomplish more on the topic together than apart, have an action agenda, contribute people or funding to the extent possible, and have the support of their agency heads. These characteristics suggest that it generally makes more sense to establish interagency groups on an as-needed basis with a specific set of issues and agenda in mind than to set up an umbrella committee. An example of such a special-purpose committee—in which BTS plays an active role—is the Federal Geographic Data Committee, which is working to standardize geographic information system (GIS) capabilities for the federal government as a whole. It may be that other special-purpose interagency committees will be useful to establish in the future (e.g., an interagency committee on the development and appropriate application of data for monitoring air quality and other environmental effects of the transportation system).

IDENTIFYING USER NEEDS

It is important for a statistical agency to obtain regular input not only on the usefulness of its current products and services (e.g., through customer surveys), but also on unmet data needs and priorities for data, indicators, analyses, and improved concepts and measures that are relevant to users' concerns. The agency must assess and interpret the input it receives—users are not always the best judges of appropriate or feasible data constructs or measures; also, they will generally want more than it is possible to provide within budget constraints. Nonetheless, user input is clearly central to the development by a statistical agency of its vision of the important information needs in its area and the characteristics of a comprehensive data system to serve those needs.

There are many constituencies for transportation data, including federal statistical and program agencies inside and outside USDOT, congressional agencies, state and local agencies, private-sector organizations, academic researchers, and the public. Input from federal agencies comes (or will come) from such activities as developing quality standards for transportation data, constructing transportation indicators, and reviewing data systems. In addition, BTS obtains input from the Advisory Council on Transportation Statistics (ACTS) (mandated in the 1991 ISTEA), which meets twice a year to consider priorities for BTS's growth and development. Although the ACTS provides a range of public- and private-sector user perspectives, its membership is small (6 people). BTS also sponsors six standing committees of the Transportation Research Board, which bring together researchers and other users to exchange information about data needs and applications in several areas (see Chapter 2). However, the transportation data community is so large and diverse that regular communication with many more users in state and local organizations, the private sector, and academia will be needed for BTS to develop and refine its vision and implementation plan for improving transportation data.

States and metropolitan planning organizations (MPOs) are particularly important constituencies for BTS to work with because of the federally based structure of planning, investment, and associated data collection and analysis for the U.S. transportation system. States and MPOs play a vital role in developing and implementing transportation policy and in making decisions about investments in transportation infrastructure that have important consequences for the cost-effectiveness of the transportation system as a whole. They also provide many key transportation data sets and, in turn, use transportation data for a wide range of purposes. A decision by Congress to devolve yet more responsibilities for transportation policy planning and implementation could further strengthen the role of states and MPOs.

BTS does not at present operate data collection systems that require working directly with states or MPOs to obtain data; such systems (e.g., the Highway Performance Monitoring System) are lodged with other USDOT modal administrations.[7] However, as the lead statistical agency for the department, BTS should develop regular channels of communication with these two important constituencies—and in the past year it has begun to do so. We recommend as a priority effort that BTS continue with its plans for obtaining regular input from states and MPOs and, relatedly, its plans for technical assistance to help states and MPOs make more effective use of transportation data (see recommendation 8 at the end of the chapter).

---

[7]See Ruddick (1996) for a comparative descriptive analysis of nine federal-state data collection systems, including the Highway Performance Monitoring System and the General Highway Statistics Program in USDOT.

Outreach to States and MPOs

BTS began over a year ago an active outreach program of meetings with state transportation officials, which were carried out in collaboration with the Office of Highway Information Management in the Federal Highway Administration and the American Association of State Highway and Transportation Officials. It then expanded these efforts to include MPOs (working through the Association of Metropolitan Planning Organizations). A conference held in spring 1997 brought together state and local officials with staff of BTS, the Federal Highway Administration, and the Federal Transit Administration to discuss priority data needs, the appropriate role of each level of government in transportation data collection and dissemination, the implications of technological advances (e.g., intelligent transportation systems) for data collection and dissemination, and the kinds of technical assistance that could help states and MPOs make more effective use of national transportation data sets.

We urge that the conference be followed up by considering the most effective communication channels to establish for regular, two-way interaction of BTS and other USDOT modal administrations with states and MPOs. Such interaction will be vitally important for BTS to carry out its mission in developing transportation indicators and filling key data gaps in its vision of a comprehensive transportation system that is relevant to user information needs.

Technical Assistance

As an outgrowth of its rounds of meetings with state transportation officials, BTS has begun to conceptualize ways to provide technical assistance to states and MPOs in obtaining, collecting, and analyzing transportation data. Technical assistance can be a draining activity for a small statistical agency, particularly if it involves one-on-one assistance on particular problems of individual organizations. However, it is possible to structure a technical assistance program so that such products as user's guides and application software are developed that have broad utility for many organizations.

In light of its mandate for intermodal data, we suggest that BTS focus its technical assistance activities on developing tools for states and MPOs for intermodal analysis, using data from BTS's two surveys, the Commodity Flow Survey (CFS) and the American Travel Survey (ATS), and other relevant sources. The 1991 ISTEA increased the planning requirements for states and MPOs, including that they consider system-wide issues instead of focusing narrowly on particular transportation modes. The ATS and the CFS, alone and linked with other information, will provide rich data sets for cross-modal analyses of transportation flows within and across states and metropolitan areas. The CFS also provides data that could be useful to states in planning future economic development (e.g., locating or further developing an airport that could be a hub for long-distance shipments of specific kinds of products).

Technical assistance in using the ATS, the CFS, and related data could take such forms as user's guides that highlight state and local applications of the data, special analysis software, and innovative methods of data analysis. Assistance could be offered in a variety of formats and venues, such as access via the Internet, continuing education classes, conferences, and, occasionally, on-site work on a particular project. Analytic tools and techniques could be developed in some cases directly by BTS, or by working with one or a few states, or through contracts with universities or other organizations.

The experience of other federal statistical agencies suggests that funding one or a few states to develop data processing and analysis tools has the advantage that other states may be more receptive to using a state-developed product (see Ruddick, 1996). If BTS uses contractors for its technical assistance activities, it is important that some BTS analysis staff also be involved, particularly in the development of analysis tools that exploit the information value of the ATS and the CFS. BTS staff need hands-on experience in using the ATS and CFS data for a variety of analysis needs in order not only to help states, MPOs, and others use the data more effectively, but also to set priorities for improving the relevance and quality of the data for the future.

ANALYSIS PROGRAMS

Data analysis is an important component of the work of a statistical agency—not only analysis of quality measures and issues related to methods, but also analysis of substantive topics. Statistical agencies should not be advocates for particular policies, but they should engage in research that sheds light on the effects of alternative policies and that illuminates trends and relationships in policy-relevant areas. Careful analyses in substantive areas that explain what the data show and qualify findings with information about the quality and appropriateness of the data for particular uses are very helpful for users. Such analyses are also critical to the statistical agency itself to help it understand the data in its area, determine how to keep the data relevant for policy and other purposes, and continually refine its vision of a comprehensive transportation data system to serve user information needs. (See Bonnen, 1997, for a discussion of the analysis roles of statistical agencies.)

Developing a substantive research program can be difficult for a statistical agency. Such research is often a target for cutbacks when budgets are tight in favor of preserving resources for data collection. Also, analytical researchers and statisticians and methodologists on the staff may not always work together effectively because of differing expertise and perspectives. Statistical agencies need to address these challenges in order to have an active in-house research program that benefits the agency and its users.

Encouraging Substantive Research

At BTS, the director has emphasized the importance of substantive research on transportation issues. The *Transportation Statistics Annual Reports* feature each year a special analytical section on a particular topic of policy concern, in addition to providing updated assessments of the state of transportation. BTS also regularly hosts seminars and conferences on research topics, and it recently inaugurated a new twice-yearly, peer-reviewed *Journal of Transportation and Statistics* that will feature research articles.

We support BTS's research initiatives and encourage an expansion of them as resources and the demands of other priorities permit. In particular, we encourage research by BTS on the substantive uses of data from the CFS and the ATS that can help policy makers understand the problems and opportunities for cost-effective intermodal transportation of people and goods.

At the same time, because research is labor-intensive and time-consuming, we urge BTS to assess how it is carrying out its research activities and whether there are more cost-effective ways to approach them. One way for BTS to augment its in-house research capabilities would be for it to announce special research initiatives in a request for proposals aimed at university faculty involved in transportation studies. Looking at the demands on its own staff, we encourage BTS to assess the contribution of the *TSARs* to the agency's analysis functions.

The Role of the *TSARs*

BTS is mandated by the 1991 ISTEA to produce a *Transportation Statistics Annual Report,* and the *TSARs* produced to date have contained useful data and analyses that were not previously available to transportation planners and analysts. However, the *TSAR* may not be the best format with which to provide transportation data analyses to the user community or, relatedly, to provide a set of widely followed national transportation indicators.

BTS is still a small agency, and the preparation of each year's *TSAR* absorbs substantial time and energy of BTS's in-house and contractor staff. Yet a thick annual report of textual chapters, even with many tables and charts, does not seem well suited to serve the information needs of policy makers and other users. They are all too likely to lose sight of the forest for the trees and to find such a publication too difficult to use, either for locating a key statistic or for understanding the relevance of trends and relationships in the data for particular policy issues and concerns.

In contrast, such publications as the monthly *Survey of Current Business*, published by the Bureau of Economic Analysis, the *Monthly Labor Review,* published by the Bureau of Labor Statistics, and the quarterly *Social Security Bulletin* regularly include standard, easily locatable tables that update key statistics. In addition, they include articles on selected topics that amplify the material in the tables. These articles may be substantive (e.g., analyzing particular trends) or related to methods (e.g., analyzing measurement problems for a particular variable). A similar monthly publication would not be feasible for BTS at its present stage of development and is likely not needed in any case, given that transportation indicators tend not to show pronounced movements over short periods of time. However, a format that provides regularly updated, standardized tables and charts of key indicators together with topical articles could be more useful and easier to produce than the *TSARs*.

We suggest that BTS consider alternative formats to the *TSARs* and that, if an alternative format seems workable, that it seek authority to adopt that format in place of the required annual report. One alternative would involve the chartbook that we earlier suggested BTS publish, together with BTS's new twice-yearly *Journal of Transportation and Statistics*.

Under this alternative, the chartbook would include 10 to 20 key statistical indicators with accompanying brief commentary and notes on methods; it would first appear annually but, as resources permit, should be published more frequently. It would be a publication that users look forward to receiving in order to follow key trends. BTS's new journal would publish not only peer-reviewed research and methods articles from BTS staff, other USDOT staff, and outside researchers, but also articles on the state of transportation containing the kind of analytical material that currently appears in the *TSARs*—perhaps in a special section covering selected topics in each issue. (As examples, an article on cross-modal trends in safety might appear every December, and an article on energy impacts of transportation might appear every June.) Our expectation is that reports on particular aspects of the transportation system (e.g., safety, access, condition of the infrastructure) that are presented in the form of journal articles will be more accessible to users than the current *TSAR* format and less burdensome on the BTS staff to develop.[8]

Together, the chartbook and the journal would fulfill the mandate in the 1991 ISTEA for BTS to provide information about the transportation system in an annual report. (In this chapter and the preceding one, we recommend several changes in BTS's roster of publications. Table 4-2 maps BTS's current publications to those that we recommend.) An alternative format that would accomplish the same goal would be to fold both the chartbook and related analytical articles into the new journal as a regularly appearing supplement. Whether this alternative is preferable to a separate chartbook depends on how often it appears useful to publish key indicators and whether the desired publication schedule could be accommodated by the journal. Under either alternative (folding both tables and analyses or just analyses into the journal), a goal for the longer term should be to

---

[8]The articles in the special section of the journal should be reviewed and held to high standards, but the review process should be managed by BTS, given its mandate to produce regular reports on the transportation system, and not by an outside editorial board.

TABLE 4-2 Bureau of Transportation Statistics Printed Periodic Publications: Current and Proposed

Publication	Current Status	Panel Proposal
Existing Periodic Publications		
Directory of Transportation Data Sources	Annual; abstracts of data sources	Continue; add information on significant features and limitations for more entries; add sample size and response rates for surveys
Journal of Transportation and Statistics	Twice yearly; peer-reviewed articles	Possibly augment with section of analytical articles on the state of the transportation system replacing the *TSARs*; also possibly augment with chartbook (see below); if augmented, seek quarterly publication as long-term goal
National Transportation Statistics (NTS)	Annual; compendium of statistical tables and charts	Continue; add explanatory notes on sources, definitions; review graphs for accurate representation
Transportation Expressions	Periodic; inventory of terms	Continue as needed
Transportation Statistics Annual Report (TSAR)	Annual; analyzes the transportation system and transportation data	Possibly replace with alternative format, such as a chartbook and section of analytical articles in the journal
New Periodic Publications		
Chartbook of 10-20 key statistical indicators		Annual at first; more frequently as needed and resources permit (perhaps include as supplement to the *Journal of Transportation and Statistics*)
Report to Congress on development of quality standards and improvements in quality of USDOT data		Every 2 years; developed through department-wide standards committee chaired by BTS; eliminates need for section on the state of transportation data in the *TSARs*
USDOT statistical budget (for data programs with significant statistical uses)		Annual; compiled by BTS for use by the secretary

publish the journal on a quarterly instead of a twice-yearly basis in order to accommodate the additional material.

Whatever publication format is adopted (one of those suggested or another), we repeat that it is important for BTS to find the most cost-effective ways by which to conduct and report the results of substantive research with its data. Such research is an essential component of a statistical agency's mission to organize, interpret, and communicate data so that the data become *information* that is relevant for policy needs and other purposes.

RECOMMENDATIONS

Vision and Plan

(5) BTS should develop a long-term strategy for implementing fully all of the areas in its mandate in order to evolve as a statistical agency that ensures the relevance, as well as the quality, of transportation data. The implementation plan should set priorities within the context of a vision of a comprehensive system of transportation data.

National Transportation Indicators

(6) BTS should develop key national statistical indicators for the transportation system—for example, multimodal series in the areas of safety, travel patterns, and the condition of the transportation infrastructure—in consultation with the statistical and analysis units in the other USDOT modal administrations and the transportation community.

USDOT Statistical Budget

(7) In the reauthorization of BTS, Congress should require BTS to compile, analyze, and provide to the secretary of transportation a department-wide statistical program budget for the secretary's use in making decisions during the budget process.

Building Relationships with States and Metropolitan Planning Organizations

(8) BTS should regularly meet with representatives from states and metropolitan planning organizations to help determine priorities for key national statistical indicators, other data, analyses, products and services, and improvements in data concepts and measurements. BTS should also provide technical advice to states and metropolitan planning organizations to help them make more effective use of BTS and other transportation data.

5

Building an Agency

To be effective over the long term in carrying out its program and mission, a statistical agency must develop a set of institutional characteristics with the strong support of its department and the Congress. It is particularly important that a statistical agency have a strong measure of professional independence; that it develop a relationship of trust with the individuals and organizations that provide data to the agency; and that it assume a leadership role in its department with regard to data quality standards, statistical methods, and related matters. All three of these institutional characteristics should be supported explicitly in legislation, through firmly established administrative procedures, and through ongoing agency practice. All three characteristics also require that the agency establish itself as a model of excellence. The agency must be held to the highest standards of performance in carrying out its program and mission, particularly its mandate to promote the quality and relevance of the data in its subject area.

We discuss below considerations in maintaining the professional independence of the Bureau of Transportation Statistics (BTS) and in developing a relationship of trust with transportation data providers. (Primary recommendations are at the end of the chapter.) Paramount in maintaining trust are credible pledges that the identity of individual reporting units will be held in confidence. We discuss the problems for BTS that are posed by data programs, such as those in the Office of Airline Information, which were developed for regulatory purposes and operate under provisions that mandate the release of data for individual businesses. Finally, we briefly review the discussion in previous chapters of the leadership role that we believe BTS should play in the statistical activities of the U.S. Department of Transportation (USDOT).

ENSURING INDEPENDENCE

In democracies, government statistical agencies have the role of providing the public and all sides in partisan debates with relevant, timely, and accurate data. Their task is to describe the status of the economy and society and to illuminate problems and the effects of policies but not to articulate solutions or to suggest policies of the government. The data from government statistical agencies must be relevant and credible to all parties in policy discussions.

In order to fulfill this role, long experience has demonstrated that statistical agencies must have a large measure of professional independence from their department and from the administration and the Congress, more broadly. They must adhere closely to their mission to collect high-quality, relevant data in order to meet the information needs of policy makers, planners, and researchers in their subject area and not stray into policy making or political analysis of their own. In turn, they must have authority to make decisions about the best way to carry out their activities so as to ensure the credibility and accuracy of the data they provide and to prevent any possibility of manipulation—or even the appearance of manipulation—of the data to serve particular political or policy purposes.

Policy makers, planners, researchers, and the public must be able to count on having data series that are produced without regard to partisan concerns or the desires of officials to enlist support for specific policies—the data must be factual and tell the story as it is. Of course, no data are without error. The key is to ensure that the data from a statistical agency not be tilted or altered in any manner to serve a particular agenda and that the data are always accompanied by information about quality and limitations.

Avoiding partisan concerns by ensuring independence in professional activities does not mean that a statistical agency should be relegated to a backwater position in its department. On the contrary, it needs to be close to the center of policy decisions if it is to keep the data in its subject area relevant and timely for policy needs and other important public purposes. Ensuring independence while encouraging relevance creates a tension that requires careful structuring of the authority, responsibility, and expectations of those involved. For example, a direct reporting line from the head of the statistical agency to the secretary of the department fosters both independence and policy relevance, so long as that reporting line carries no requirement or expectation that the statistical agency will submit its data releases for prior approval regarding content or date of release. (The secretary of transportation has been scrupulous about respecting BTS's independence in this regard.) It is important that the statistical agency be seen by its department as professionally competent and that the head of the statistical agency provide apolitical advice on the basis of the agency's knowledge of the data it compiles.

Current Protections for BTS Independence

The 1991 Intermodal Surface Transportation Efficiency Act (ISTEA) protects the professional independence of BTS in two important ways. First, it establishes BTS as a separate agency within USDOT. Second, it provides for an independent, professionally qualified agency head. Specifically, it stipulates that the BTS director:

- "shall be appointed by the President, with the advice and consent of the Senate . . . from among individuals who are qualified . . . by virtue of their training and experience in the compilation and analysis of transportation statistics";
- "shall report directly to the Secretary [of Transportation]"; and that
- "the term of the Director shall be 4 years."

In setting up BTS as a separate modal administration in USDOT, the department carried out the ISTEA mandate for an independent statistical agency in which the director reports directly to the secretary. The department also nominated a highly qualified individual to serve as the first director. In addition, the department has helped to ensure BTS's professional independence by establishing practices whereby BTS has the authority to select and promote its professional staff and to release statistical information without prior clearance. BTS seeks wide review inside the department of such publications as the *Transportation Statistics Annual Report*. However, the comments it receives are advisory; BTS does not have to accept them nor to hold up publication awaiting them.[1] Finally, the department has supported the analytical programs in which BTS has sought to make clear that it is not engaged in policy analysis of the kind in which particular policy options are developed or recommended. Rather, its analytical work is intended to help policy analysts and other users understand what the data have to say about trends in transportation, including the effects of policies, and the possible implications for future policy making. The current BTS director has established a good record in this regard.

Looking to the Future

We recommend that the formal and informal mechanisms now in place to ensure BTS's professional independence be strengthened and expanded (see recommendation 9 at the end of the chapter). First, the ISTEA provisions for an independent, qualified director of BTS should be reiterated in the reauthorization of BTS. In addition, the reauthorization should confirm BTS's existing authority to release statistical information without prior approval by political officials out-

---

[1] The 1991 ISTEA specifies the *Transportation Statistics Annual Report* as a report from the director of BTS to the President and Congress.

side BTS. No problems have arisen in this regard in the past, but BTS is a new agency that has not yet had time to develop all of its mandated functions. As BTS expands its programs and functions (e.g., begins to publish key national indicators), we believe that statutory confirmation of its authority to release statistical information without prior approval is advisable.

We also urge that BTS staffing levels, as well as budget amounts, be approved through the normal budget process, involving discussions between BTS and the department, the U.S. Office of Management and Budget, and, ultimately, the Congress. At present, BTS dollar levels are set in the 1991 ISTEA for the 6-year period of authorization, with yearly review and approval by the department, the Office of Management and Budget, and the Congress. However, BTS staffing levels have, at times, been subject to ad hoc decisions by the secretary to reallocate full-time-equivalent (FTE) positions within the department. Thus, in mid-1996, the Office of the Secretary made a decision to lower the approved FTE ceiling for BTS from 75 to 60 positions through fiscal 1997, even though BTS had adequate budget to support the higher number. BTS must be able to develop long-range plans for both its expenditure levels and the number, types, and caliber of its technical staff.

Another way in which the department can support BTS's professional independence concerns press releases. The practice varies widely across cabinet departments as to whether the department, a component of the department, or the statistical agency is featured in a press release about the agency's data (e.g., the statistical agency is featured in the press releases of the Energy Information Administration). Because BTS needs to become established as a strong, credible agency that assumes responsibility for the data it produces, we urge the department to list BTS on the masthead of press releases about BTS's data, in contrast to the current practice, in which BTS's name appears only in the text. (BTS press releases should also include information about the quality of the data being released.) Further, when BTS begins to develop regularly published indicators of the transportation system, it will be important to establish predetermined schedules of public release in order to prevent the manipulation or the appearance of manipulation of release dates for political or policy purposes.

Yet another way in which the department, the administration, and the Congress can help ensure the professional independence of BTS and, more generally, its ability to evolve into an effective statistical agency is to act expeditiously in the matter of appointing (or reappointing) a director for the agency at the end of each 4-year term. It is detrimental to an agency's morale and to its ability to move forward with an agenda to have to endure a period in which there is no designated director. Inevitably, plans are put on hold and momentum is lost, which can be particularly damaging for a new agency that is trying to build its staff and reputation. (In May 1997, the U.S. Senate confirmed the reappointment of the first BTS director, T.R. Lakshmanan, to a second 4-year term.)

Similarly, it is helpful for the evolution of a statistical agency to have a measure of stability from a statute that authorizes the agency on a permanent or long-term basis. (At present, all of the major statistical agencies are permanently authorized, with the exception of the National Center for Health Statistics, which must be reauthorized every 5 to 6 years, and BTS itself, which was initially authorized for a 6-year period in the 1991 ISTEA.) With the knowledge that its existence is ensured over a long period, an agency is in a better position to work toward such long-range goals as building a strong statistical staff, developing a culture of commitment to data quality, and constructing high-quality, relevant statistical indicators.

BUILDING TRUST

To maintain credibility and be able to obtain the cooperation of respondents to surveys and other data collection programs, a statistical agency must have a relationship of trust with data providers. Key to maintaining this relationship are procedures and practices that provide a firm guarantee of confidentiality of responses—specifically, that no data will be released that could identify an individual person or business. Other practices, such as informing respondents of the anticipated uses of the information, designing data collection so as to minimize reporting burden, seeking opportunities to assist data providers to make use of the data they have themselves provided, and obtaining input from respondents (and others) in planning the scope of data collection and data products, are also helpful in building trust (see National Research Council, 1992b, and Appendix C).

We focus on the issue of maintaining the confidentiality of responses from individuals and businesses. The critical nature of confidentiality protection for the mission of a statistical agency and the implications for the kinds of data programs the agency should operate is particularly important to address in a department like USDOT that has many data systems that serve administrative and regulatory functions in which identification of reporting units is an operational necessity.

Confidentiality Protection

The release of data that identify individual reporting units is incompatible with the mission of a statistical agency.[2] A statistical agency provides data, not for administrative, regulatory, or enforcement purposes, which would require the identification of individual respondents, but for description, evaluation, and analysis on the basis of patterns and trends from groups of respondents (National Re-

---

[2]The exception is when the reporting units, such as state and local governments, are public entities, in which case statistical agencies commonly report data for individual units (e.g., highway expenditures of each state) as well as for groups (e.g., expenditures by budget category for cities grouped by population size class). However, the emphasis in such reporting is always on data that are useful for policy planning, evaluation, and research, not for investigation or auditing.

search Council, 1992b:2). Statistics by definition pertain to groups and not to individual units.

Also, statistical agencies must generally rely on the voluntary cooperation of respondents to obtain high-quality data. Such cooperation may be impaired if respondents believe that the data they provide will be released in a way that identifies them to others. Although the research literature in this area is scant, a few studies have found that response rates to surveys, particularly to such sensitive items as income, are somewhat lower when there is not a strong assurance of confidentiality. Also, surveys of taxpayers find that, although many people are willing to have their tax records shared with other agencies for specific purposes, large minorities of taxpayers are opposed to any type of data sharing (see National Research Council, 1993:80-85). Furthermore, statistical agencies that conduct establishment surveys frequently find that businesses are reluctant to respond because of concerns that sensitive information will be identifiable and hence available to competitors.

Protection of confidentiality does not require that data must always be released in aggregate form. Many statistical agencies release microdata files as well as aggregate statistics. Microdata files are very useful to researchers, enabling them to produce statistics and analyses to suit their particular purposes. However, statistical microdata files, although they provide data for individual reporting units, do so in a manner that guards against disclosure of the identity of a unit—for example, such files carry no name or address, have limited geographic identification, and alter sensitive variables that might otherwise possibly permit disclosure (e.g., reported income above a specified amount may be assigned to a single broad category). Also, microdata files are samples of reporting units (either from a sample survey or a sample of census records), which further protects confidentiality.[3]

The 1991 ISTEA recognized the importance of confidentiality protection for data provided by BTS. It contains an explicit prohibition on certain disclosures (see Appendix A):

> Information compiled by the Bureau shall not be disclosed publicly in a manner that would reveal the personal identity of any individual . . . or to reveal trade secrets or allow commercial or financial information provided by any person to be identified with such person.

We recommend that the reauthorization of BTS include an explicit provision that it not release information that would identify individuals or businesses in its surveys and other data collection programs (see recommendation 10 at the end of

---

[3]When a statistical agency believes that it is not possible to release microdata files with sufficient data for analysis in a form that protects against disclosure, other arrangements may be made for research use of the microdata. For example, the Census Bureau has recently established two secure Research Data Centers (one at its Boston regional office and the other at Carnegie Mellon University) for access to its longitudinal research database on manufacturing establishments. Researchers must come to the center, be sworn as special Census Bureau agents, and use the data on site.

the chapter). Furthermore, BTS should make clear its commitment to protecting confidentiality in its publications and in information that accompanies its CD-ROMs and other data products.

Identifiable Data from Regulatory Systems

Many data systems in USDOT are operated for administrative, regulatory, and enforcement purposes in which it is necessary to identify individual reporting units. Such data may not be publicly available on a routine basis, but the data are potentially available in identifiable form through such means as documentation for regulatory hearings and judicial proceedings. Moreover, such data provide the basis for enforcement actions against particular reporting units. As an example, the Federal Aviation Administration maintains large operational databases that provide the basis for grounding or requiring changes in operations of particular airlines that violate safety standards and procedures.

A statistical agency cannot operate data programs for which there can be no guarantee of confidentiality protection and that may be used to sanction individuals or businesses or take other actions that affect them directly. It would no longer be a statistical agency and could not maintain its credibility with respondents or its reputation as a nonpartisan source of objective data for policy making, planning, and research. However, there are many ways in which a statistical agency can contribute to the administrative and regulatory data programs in a department without becoming directly involved in their operation.

A statistical agency can provide technical advice on data collection and processing, for example, on the design of reporting forms and instruments and efficient methods of data processing.[4] It can also provide technical assistance in the analysis of the data to identify patterns that could be helpful for consistent regulation and enforcement. Finally, a statistical agency can serve as the compiler and disseminator of statistical reports and data products from the administrative or regulatory data. This function is particularly useful when there is no requirement that individually identifiable data be released on a routine basis. When there is such release, users can develop their own aggregate statistics; however, it may still be useful for a statistical agency to produce aggregate reports of key time series or other broadly relevant statistics. (In Box 5-1, we illustrate ways in which statistical agencies contribute to the *statistical* use of administrative and regulatory data through an example from another area—income tax returns.)

We believe that, as BTS develops its statistical staff and gains stature in the department, it can be increasingly helpful to the other modal administrations in USDOT by providing technical assistance, not only for statistical data programs (e.g., surveys), but also for regulatory and administrative data. However, BTS

---

[4]For example, in the area of pension regulation, the Bureau of Labor Statistics has advised the Pension and Welfare Benefits Administration on efficient methods for processing the information that private employers are required to provide about enrollment and funding of pension plans.

BOX 5-1
Statistical Uses of Individual Income Tax Return Data

Internal Revenue Service (IRS)

Processes individual and corporate income tax return data to calculate taxes and refunds, monitor compliance, and take action against fraud and delinquency. Tax return data are not routinely made available for individual tax filing units (whether people or businesses), but they are potentially available to enforcement agencies (e.g., the Justice Department) and for court proceedings. Includes a statistical unit (see below).

Statistics of Income (SOI) program in IRS

Statistical enclave within IRS that prepares statistical microdata files of samples of individual tax returns and publications of aggregate individual and corporate income tax data for policy analysis and research use. SOI provides a detailed microdata file of a sample of individual tax returns to the Office of Tax Analysis in the Treasury Department and the Joint Committee on Taxation for use in simulating the likely effects on government revenues of proposed changes to tax laws. (This file lacks identifying information, such as name and address, but contains complete tax filing information for each sample tax return.) SOI prepares a public-use microdata file that is elaborately processed to protect confidentiality (e.g., tax returns for high-income filing units are subsampled, state and local income tax deductions are blurred). SOI supports statistical methods research in such areas as the development of longitudinal samples and of samples that permit early publication of estimates when not all returns have been processed. SOI has no involvement with tax administration or enforcement.

Census Bureau

Uses public-use SOI microdata file for estimating after-tax income of survey respondents. Obtains limited confidential data from SOI on individual income tax filing units (e.g., type of filing unit, number of exemptions) to use in estimating migration rates between local areas for developing small-area population estimates between censuses. Also obtains limited confidential income information (e.g., wages and salaries) for evaluating the quality of reporting in household surveys. Obtains address information from corporate income tax returns with which to develop a list of the universe of business establishments (the Standard Statistical Establishment List) for use in business censuses and surveys. Also obtains selected information from returns for small businesses to reduce their reporting requirements in surveys. No confidential IRS data are publicly released in any form by the Census Bureau.

Bureau of Economic Analysis

Uses aggregate IRS data as input to the National Income and Product Accounts.

should not operate data programs for which there can be no guarantee of confidentiality protection—which raises a problem, because two such programs were recently assigned to BTS. These programs—those of the Office of Airline Information and the Motor Carrier Statistics Program—were originally regulatory in nature. With financial deregulation of transportation industries, the data, for the most part, no longer serve regulatory purposes, but the programs continue to provide for routine release of information for individual carriers. We briefly review these programs and the implications for BTS in the next section

BTS Data Programs that Release Identifiable Data

Office of Airline Information

BTS currently houses the Office of Airline Information (OAI), which operates data programs that were developed by the Civil Aeronautics Board when that agency regulated the airline industry with respect to entry, pricing, and related matters. The airlines were deregulated in 1978, but the data programs continued under provisions in the *Code of Federal Regulations* that specify reporting requirements for the airlines and the availability of data series. Many of the OAI data series are publicly available not only as aggregated statistics, but also in a form that identifies individual airlines. Major data sets and their availability include the following:

- *Domestic operations by segment of service for large and small certificated U.S. air carriers* Airlines provide monthly information on passengers (by class), freight, and mail that boarded and deboarded flights on each segment of travel (e.g., New York-Chicago) for each type of aircraft (e.g., Boeing 727). These data, which identify individual airlines, are available on an unrestricted basis to all users.
- *International operations by segment of service for U.S. and foreign carriers* The international operations data are similar to the domestic operations data, but they are restricted (i.e., available in identifiable form only upon application and by agreeing not to share the data with others) for a specified time period after collection. The restriction period is currently 6 months (prior to March 1997, it was 3 years), after which time the data are available in identifiable form to all users.
- *Financial data on large and small certificated U.S. air carriers* Airlines report quarterly data on profit and loss, balance sheets, and operating expenses. These data are similar to what public companies are required to report to the Securities and Exchange Commission (SEC), and like reports to the SEC, they are available in identifiable form on an unrestricted basis.[5]

---

[5]Commuter air carriers provide more limited flight operation and financial data on a quarterly basis. For some small carriers, the financial data are available in identifiable form only on a restricted basis (i.e., only upon application and by agreeing not to share the data with others).

• *Origin and destination data from a 10 percent sample of tickets* The ticket information (collected quarterly from the airlines) includes origin and destination for each stage of an air trip, airline, class, and ticket price. The full data set is available only on a restricted basis as defined previously (with no time limit); the data set without prices is available on an unrestricted basis.

The OAI data are used for many purposes: by the Office of the Secretary to award international routes to domestic airlines (the one area in which the government retains a regulatory role); by the Transportation and Justice Departments to monitor domestic airline competitive status and behavior; by the Federal Aviation Administration to allocate such resources as funding for airport expansion and number of inspectors at each airport; by the Defense Department to determine the health of the airlines; and by the General Accounting Office to conduct studies of the airline industry requested by the Congress. The data are also heavily used by the airlines themselves to identify targets of opportunity for expansion, to readjust routes and schedules, and for similar purposes.

Motor Carrier Statistics Program

Recently, BTS was assigned yet another data program that provides individually identifiable information: the Motor Carrier Statistics Program, which obtains financial and operating information from large interstate freight and passenger motor carriers. These data, which were originally developed by the now-defunct Interstate Commerce Commission, are currently available for individual carriers. (Data for individual bus lines are provided on the BTS web site.)

The legislation that transferred the Motor Carrier Statistics Program to USDOT required the department to evaluate and redesign the program to take account of data users' needs (particularly for data that are relevant to safety concerns), the need to preserve confidential business information, and the need to reduce reporting burden. BTS recently issued a notice *(Federal Register,* December 9, 1996:64849-64851) of the process it intends to follow to evaluate and redesign the Motor Carrier Statistics Program.

Implications for BTS

Given that a statistical agency is not an administrative, regulatory, or enforcement agency and that central to its mission is a commitment not to release individually identifiable data, we are concerned about the placement of the Office of Airline Information and the Motor Carrier Statistics Program within BTS. The continued operation of data programs within BTS that require release of data in identifiable form poses a risk to the evolution of BTS as a statistical agency that can credibly pledge confidentiality to survey respondents. We believe this risk is present even when the reporting units themselves generally support full disclosure and the data are not used for enforcement (as is true of the OAI data programs).

We recommend that BTS evaluate the OAI and Motor Carrier Statistics programs from the perspective of their compatibility with its mission as a statistical agency (see recommendation 11 at the end of the chapter). The review should establish whether it is necessary to the continued effective use of the data that they be released in individually identifiable form. From the many public- and private-sector uses of the data provided by OAI for individual airlines, there are likely strong arguments to continue to make them available on that basis. In the case of the Motor Carrier Statistics program, it may be that the data can be useful without such identification. If a determination is made that the data in one or both of these programs need to be made available in identifiable form in order to serve important public purposes, then BTS should recommend to the secretary of transportation that the programs be transferred elsewhere in USDOT for operation. BTS should continue to be as helpful as possible in improving the quality and usefulness of the data. It should also incorporate statistics derived from the data in its electronic and printed products and use the data as appropriate to develop indicators, but it should not operate the programs so long as there are provisions to release the data for individual reporting units.

ATTAINING LEADERSHIP

As the statistical agency in USDOT with a broad mandate to improve transportation data, BTS should have leadership responsibilities in such areas as developing department-wide data quality standards and coordinating the collection of transportation data with agencies inside and outside USDOT. BTS will need to develop its staff capabilities to carry out these responsibilities and to be able to assume leadership in fact and not just in name. It will also need to focus its attention on data quality and relevance more than on quantity of data and services and to set priorities so as to make the most of its available resources.

Both formal and informal means of support will be needed for BTS to develop an appropriate leadership role in the department. Thus, we recommended (in Chapter 3) that the reauthorization of BTS strengthen its mandate to develop binding data quality standards for USDOT. We also recommended (in Chapter 4) that the department assign BTS the responsibility to develop a statistical budget that can help identify data priorities and assist the secretary in making budget decisions about USDOT data programs.

Even with strengthened authority, BTS is not likely to have an easy time in developing stature in USDOT in such areas as standards setting and coordination of data collection. Asserting leadership will be particularly difficult when it appears that the mission or budget of one or more modal administrations may be affected—for example, if there is a proposal to integrate previously separate data collection programs into what could be a more cost-effective combined program.

BTS will need strong ongoing support from the Office of the Secretary, particularly while it is still building its staff capabilities and developing excellence in its own operations. In turn, BTS must achieve high standards of performance so that it can gain the reputation necessary for a leadership role. Finally, BTS and the department should seek opportunities to develop such programs as staff exchanges between BTS and statistical units in the other modal administrations. These kinds of programs can foster good working relationships and promote cooperative efforts to improve the quality and relevance of transportation data for the benefit of the entire community of transportation data users.

RECOMMENDATIONS

Ensuring Independence

(9) The reauthorization of BTS should continue the provisions of current law that the director of BTS be a presidential appointee with a fixed term of 4 years, who reports directly to the secretary of transportation and is a qualified professional with relevant training and experience. The reauthorization should underscore the professional independence of BTS by statutorily confirming its authority to release statistical information without prior clearance by political officials outside BTS.

Protecting Confidentiality

(10) The reauthorization of BTS should continue to require that it not release data that could identify individual or business respondents.

(11) BTS should review the Office of Airline Information and Motor Carrier Statistics programs, which provide for the release of individually identifiable data, for their compatibility with the BTS mission as a statistical agency that is committed to confidentiality protection. To the extent that the data from these programs need to be available in identifiable form to serve important policy purposes, BTS should recommend to the secretary that the programs be lodged elsewhere in USDOT.

Acronyms Used in the Report

AASHTO	American Association of State Highway and Transportation Officials
ATS	American Travel Survey
BEA	Bureau of Economic Analysis
BJS	Bureau of Justice Statistics
BLS	Bureau of Labor Statistics
BTS	Bureau of Transportation Statistics
CD-ROM	Compact Disk - Read Only Memory
CEX	Consumer Expenditure Survey
CFR	Code of Federal Regulations
CFS	Commodity Flow Survey
CNSTAT	Committee on National Statistics
CTPP	Census Transportation Planning Package
EIA	Energy Information Administration
EPA	Environmental Protection Agency
FAA	Federal Aviation Administration
FARS	Fatal Accident Reporting System
FGDC	Federal Geographic Data Committee
FHWA	Federal Highway Administration
FTE	Full-Time Equivalent
FRA	Federal Railroad Administration
FTA	Federal Transit Administration

GDP	Gross Domestic Product
GES	General Estimates System
GIS	Geographic Information System
GNP	Gross National Product
HPMS	Highway Performance Monitoring System
ICC	Interstate Commerce Commission
ISTEA	Intermodal Surface Transportation Efficiency Act (1991)
MARAD	Maritime Administration
MPO	Metropolitan Planning Organization
MSA	Metropolitan Statistical Area
NAFTA	North American Free Trade Agreement
NAPA	National Academy of Public Administration
NAS	National Academy of Sciences
NASS	National Agricultural Statistics Service
NASS	National Accident Sampling System
NCES	National Center for Education Statistics
NCHS	National Center for Health Statistics
NHTSA	National Highway Traffic Safety Administration
NIPA	National Income and Product Accounts
NPR	National Performance Review
NPTS	Nationwide Personal Transportation Survey
NRC	National Research Council
NTDB	National Transit Data Base
NTL	National Transportation Library
NTS	*National Transportation Statistics*
O & D	Origin and Destination
OAI	Office of Airline Information
OHIM	Office of Highway Information Management
OMB	(U.S.) Office of Management and Budget
OST	Office of the Secretary of Transportation
PIERS	Port Import Export Reporting System
RSPA	Research and Special Programs Administration
RTECS	Residential Transportation Energy Consumption Survey
SES	Senior Executive Service
SMART	State and Metropolitan Analysis for Regional Transportation
SLSDC	St. Lawrence Seaway Development Corporation
SOI	Statistics of Income program
TDC	Transportation Data Center

TRB	Transportation Research Board
TSA	Transportation Satellite Account
TSAR	*Transportation Statistics Annual Report*
USCG	United States Coast Guard
USDOT	United States Department of Transportation

References

Australian Bureau of Statistics
    1990   Data quality. Section 3.3 in *ABS Publishing Manual*. Canberra: Australian Bureau of Statistics.

Bonnen, James T.
    1977   Assessment of the current agricultural data base: An information system approach. Pp. 386-407 in Lee R. Martin et al., eds., *A Survey of Agricultural Economics Literature*. Vol. 2. Minneapolis: University of Minnesota Press.
    1983   Federal statistical coordination: A disaster or a disgrace. *American Statistician* 37(3):179-192, 199-202.
    1996   The politics of statistical reform: A cautionary tale, 1978-1980. *Chance* 9(1):17-26.
    1997   *The Changing Relationship of Statistical Data and Analysis*. Department of Agricultural Economics Staff Paper 97-17 (April). Lansing: Michigan State University.

Bureau of the Census
    1991   *Survey of Income and Program Participation Users' Guide*. 2nd edition. Washington, D.C.: U.S. Department of Commerce.
    1992   *Census of Population and Housing 1990: Public Use Microdata Sample U.S. Technical Documentation*. Washington, D.C.: U.S. Department of Commerce.
    1996a   *1992 Census of Transportation, Communications, and Utilities: 1993 Commodity Flow Survey California*. Report #TC92-CF-5. Washington, D.C.: U.S. Department of Commerce.
    1996b   *Statistical Abstract of the United States 1996*. 116th Edition. Washington, D.C.: U.S. Department of Commerce.

Bureau of Economic Analysis
    1995   Mid-decade strategic review of BEA's economic accounts: Maintaining and improving their performance. *Survey of Current Business* February:37-66.

Bureau of Economic Analysis-Bureau of Transportation Statistics Working Group
    1996   *Transportation Satellite Account: Overview and Progress Report*. Report prepared for Charles A. Waite (September). BEA (Bureau of Economic Analysis)-BTS (Bureau of Transportation Statistics) Working Group. Washington, D.C.: U.S. Departments of Commerce and Transportation.

REFERENCES

Bureau of Labor Statistics
   1992   *BLS Handbook of Methods*. Bulletin 2414 (September). Washington, D.C.: U.S. Department of Labor.

Bureau of Transportation Statistics
   1993a   *Directory of Transportation Data Sources*. Issued annually beginning in 1993. Washington, D.C.: U.S. Department of Transportation.
   1993b   *National Transportation Statistics*. Issued annually under BTS beginning in 1993. Washington, D.C.: U.S. Department of Transportation.
   1993c   *Purpose and Status of the Multimodal Commodity and Passenger Flow Surveys*. Report to the Committees on Appropriations of the U.S. Senate and U.S. House of Representatives. Washington, D.C.: U.S. Department of Transportation.
   1994a   *Transportation Expressions*. Washington, D.C.: U.S. Department of Transportation. [also issued 1996]
   1994b   *Transportation Statistics Annual Report*. Issued annually beginning in 1994. Washington, D.C.: U.S. Department of Transportation.
   1995   *Transportation Statistics Annual Report*. Washington, D.C.: U.S. Department of Transportation.
   1996a   *Implications of Continuous Measurement for the Uses of Census Data in Transportation Planning*. Washington, D.C.: U.S. Department of Transportation.
   1996b   *Transportation Statistics Annual Report*. Washington, D.C.: U.S. Department of Transportation.

Cleveland, William
   1985   *The Elements of Graphing Data*. Monterey, Calif.: Wadsworth Advanced Books and Software.
   1993   *Visualizing Data*. Murray Hill, N.J.: Hobart Press.

Council of Professional Associations on Federal Statistics
   1997   *News from COPAFS* (January-March). Alexandria, Va.: Council of Professional Associations on Federal Statistics.

Duncan, Joseph W., and William C. Shelton
   1978   *Revolution in United States Government Statistics, 1926-1976*. Office of Federal Statistical Policy and Standards. Washington, D.C.: U.S. Department of Commerce.

Energy Information Administration
   no date   *The Energy Information Standards Manual*. Washington, D.C. U.S. Department of Energy.
   1996   *Residential Energy Consumption Survey Quality Profile*. DOE/EIA-0555(96)/1. Washington, D.C.: U.S. Department of Energy.

Executive Office of the President
   1997a   *Budget of the United States Government, Fiscal Year 1998. Appendix*. Washington, D.C.: Executive Office of the President.
   1997b   *Statistical Programs of the United States Government, Fiscal Year 1997*. Office of Management and Budget. Washington, D.C.: Executive Office of the President.

Flemming, Emmett, Jr.
   1992   *NCES Statistical Standards*. Statistical Standards and Methodology Division, National Center for Education Statistics. NCES Report #92-102. Washington, D.C.: U.S. Department of Education.

Freedman, Harry, Jim Booth, Jean-Francois Gosselin, Shaila Nijhowne, and Innis Sande
   1987   *Quality Guidelines*. 2nd edition (April). Ottawa: Statistics Canada.

Groves, Robert M.
   1995   Challenges of methodological innovation in government statistical agencies. Pp. 45-79 in Z. Kenessey, ed., *The Future of Statistics: An International Perspective*. Netherlands: Editions Voorborg.

Jabine, Thomas B.
  1994 *Quality Profile for SASS: Aspects of the Quality of Data in Schools and Staffing Surveys.* National Center for Education Statistics, Office of Educational Research and Improvement. NCES Report #94-340. Washington, D.C.: U.S. Department of Education.

Jabine, Thomas B., Karen E. King, and Rita J. Petroni
  1990 *Survey of Income and Program Participation: Quality Profile.* Bureau of the Census. Washington, D.C.: U.S. Department of Commerce.

Mitroff, Ian I., Richard O. Mason, and Vincent P. Barabba
  1983 *The 1980 Census: Policymaking Amid Turbulence.* Lexington, Mass.: Lexington Books.

National Academy of Public Administration
  1991 *Organizing the Administration of Surface Transportation Policies and Programs to Meet National Needs.* Washington, D.C.: National Academy of Public Administration.

National Research Council
  1990 *Data Requirements for Monitoring Truck Safety.* Special Report 228. Committee for the Truck Safety Data Needs Study, Transportation Research Board, National Research Council. Washington, D.C.: Transportation Research Board.
  1992a *Data for Decisions: Requirements for National Transportation Policy Making.* Special Report 234. Committee for the Study of Strategic Transportation Data Needs, Transportation Research Board, National Research Council. Washington, D.C.: Transportation Research Board.
  1992b *Principles and Practices for a Federal Statistical Agency.* Margaret E. Martin and Miron L. Straf, eds. Committee on National Statistics, National Research Council. Washington, D.C.: National Academy Press.
  1993 *Private Lives and Public Policies: Confidentiality and Accessibility of Government Statistics.* George T. Duncan, Thomas B. Jabine, and Virginia A. de Wolf, eds. Panel on Confidentiality and Data Access, Committee on National Statistics, National Research Council. Washington, D.C.: National Academy Press.

Norwood, Janet L.
  1995 *Organizing to Count: Change in the Federal Statistical System.* Washington, D.C.: The Urban Institute Press.

Ruddick, Michelle M.
  1996 Characteristics of Federal-State Data Collection Systems: Perspectives from Federal and State Agencies. Working paper prepared for the Panel on Statistical Programs and Practices of the Bureau of Transportation Statistics, Committee on National Statistics and Transportation Research Board, National Research Council, Washington, D.C.

Sirken, Monroe G., B. Iris Shimizu, Dwight K. French, and Dwight B. Brock
  1992 *Manual on Standards and Procedures for Reviewing Statistical Reports.* National Center for Health Statistics, Centers for Disease Control. Washington, D.C.: U.S. Department of Health and Human Services.

Statistics Canada
  1992 Policy on informing users of data quality and methodology. In *Policy Manual* (April 7). Ottawa: Statistics Canada.

Statistics Sweden
  1994 *Quality Definition and Recommendations for Quality Declarations of Official Statistics.* Reports on Statistical Coordination (April). Stockholm: Statistics Sweden.

Tufte, Edward
  1983 *The Visual Display of Quantitative Information.* Cheshire, Conn.: Graphics Press.

U.S. Department of Education
  1988 *Organization Review Program: A Report on Five Federal Statistical Organizations.* Office of Management, Management Improvement Service. Prepared for the National Center for Education Statistics. Washington, D.C.: U.S. Department of Education.

U.S. Department of Transportation
   1990   *Statement of National Transportation Policy.* Washington, D.C.: U.S. Department of Transportation.

Young, Allan H.
   1996   Reliability and accuracy of quarterly GDP Estimates: A review. Pp. 423-449 in John W. Kendrick, ed., *The New System of National Accounts.* Boston: Kluwer Academic Publishers.

APPENDICES

APPENDIX
A

The Intermodal Surface Transportation Efficiency Act of 1991: References to the Bureau of Transportation Statistics

PL 102-240—DECEMBER 18, 1991

Sec. 6006. Bureau of Transportation Statistics.
(105 Stat. 2172)

Chapter I of title 49, United States Code, is amended by adding at the end the following new section:

"Sec. 111. Bureau of Transportation Statistics.

"(a) Establishment.-There is established in the Department of Transportation a Bureau of Transportation Statistics.

"(b) Director.-

(1) Appointment.-The Bureau shall be headed by a Director who shall be appointed by the President, by and with the advice and consent of the Senate.
(2) Qualifications.-The Director shall be appointed from among individuals who are qualified to serve as the Director by virtue of their training and experience in the compilation and analysis of transportation statistics.
(3) Reporting.-The Director shall report directly to the Secretary.
(4) Term.-The term of the Director shall be 4 years. The term of the first Director to be appointed shall begin on the 180th day after the date of the enactment of this section.

"(c) Responsibilities.-The Director of the Bureau shall be responsible for carrying out the following duties:

(1) Compiling transportation statistics.-Compiling, analyzing, and publishing a comprehensive set of transportation statistics to provide timely summaries and totals (including industrywide aggregates and multiyear averages) of transportation-related information. Such statistics shall be suitable for conducting cost-benefit studies (including comparisons among individual transportation modes and intermodal transport systems) and shall include information on-

(A) productivity in various parts of the transportation sector;
(B) traffic flows;
(C) travel times;
(D) vehicle weights;
(E) variables influencing traveling behavior, including choice of transportation mode;
(F) travel costs of intracity commuting and intercity trips;
(G) availability of mass transit and the number of passengers served by each mass transit authority;
(H) frequency of vehicle and transportation facility repairs and other interruptions of transportation service;
(I) accidents;
(J) collateral damage to the human and natural environment; and
(K) the condition of the transportation system.

(2) Implementing long-term data collection program.-Establishing and implementing, in cooperation with the modal administrators, the States, and other Federal officials a comprehensive, long-term program for the collection and analysis of data relating to the performance of the national transportation system. Such program shall-

(A) be coordinated with efforts to develop performance indicators for the national transportation system undertaken pursuant to section 307(b)(3) of title 23, United States Code;
(B) ensure that data is collected under this subsection in a manner which will maximize the ability to compare data from different regions and for different time periods; and
(C) ensure that data collected under this subsection is controlled for accuracy and disseminated to the States and other interested parties.

(3) Issuing guidelines.-Issuing guidelines for the collection of information by the Department of Transportation required for statistics to be compiled under paragraph (1) in order to ensure that such information is accurate, reliable, relevant, and in a form that permits systematic analysis.

(4) Coordinating collection of information.-Coordinating the collection of information by the Department of Transportation required for statistics to be compiled under paragraph (1) with related information-gathering activities conducted by other Federal departments and agencies and collecting appropriate data not elsewhere gathered.

(5) Making statistics accessible.-Making the statistics published under this subsection readily accessible.

(6) Identifying information needs.-Identifying information that is needed under paragraph (1) but which is not being collected, reviewing such needs at least annually with the Advisory Council on Transportation Statistics, and making recommendations to appropriate Department of Transportation research officials concerning extramural and intramural research programs to provide such information.

"(d) Limitations on Statutory Construction.-Nothing in this section shall be construed-

(1) to authorize the Bureau to require any other department or agency to collect data; or

(2) to reduce the authority of any other officer of the Department of Transportation to collect and disseminate data independently.

"(e) Prohibition on Certain Disclosures.-Information compiled by the Bureau shall not be disclosed publicly in a manner that would reveal the personal identity of any individual, consistent with the Privacy Act of 1974 (5 U.S.C. 552a), or to reveal trade secrets or allow commercial or financial information provided by any person to be identified with such person.

"(f) Transportation Statistics Annual Report.-On or before January 1, 1994, and annually thereafter, the Director shall transmit to the President and Congress a Transportation Statistics Annual Report which shall include information on items referred to in subsection (c) (1), documentation of methods used to obtain and ensure the quality of the statistics presented in the report, and recommendations for improving transportation statistical information.

"(g) Performance of Functions of Director Pending Confirmation.-An individual who, on the date of the enactment of this section, is performing any function required by this section to be performed by the Director may continue to perform such function until such function is undertaken by the Director.

(b) Funding.-There shall be available from the Highway Trust Fund (other than the Mass Transit Account) only for carrying out the amendment made by subsection (a) $5,000,000 for fiscal year 1992, $10,000,000 for fiscal year 1993, $15,000,000 per fiscal year for each of fiscal years 1994 and 1995, $20,000,000 for fiscal year 1996, and $25,000,000 for fiscal year 1997. Funds authorized by this subsection shall be available for obligation in the same manner as if such funds were apportioned under chapter 1 of title 23, United States Code.

(c) Conforming Amendment.-The analysis for chapter 1 of such title is amended by adding at the end the following new items:

"Sec. 110. Saint Lawrence Seaway Development Corporation.

"Sec. 111. Bureau of Transportation Statistics."

(d) Amendment to Title 5, U.S.C.-Section 5316 of title 5, United States Code, is amended by adding at the end the following:

Director, Bureau of Transportation Statistics."

Sec. 6007. Advisory Council on Transportation Statistics.
(105 Stat. 2174)

(a) Establishment.-The Director of the Bureau of Transportation Statistics shall establish an Advisory Council on Transportation Statistics.

(b) Function.-It shall be the function of the advisory council established under this section to advise the Director of the Bureau of Transportation Statistics on transportation statistics and analyses, including whether or not the statistics and analysis disseminated by the Bureau of Transportation Statistics are of high quality and are based upon the best available objective information.

(c) Membership.-The advisory council established under this section shall be composed of not more than 6 members appointed by the Director who are not officers or employees of the United States and who (except for 1 member who shall have expertise in economics and 1 member who shall have expertise in statistics) have expertise in transportation statistics and analysis.

(d) Applicability of Federal Advisory Committee Act.-The Federal Advisory Committee Act shall apply to the advisory council established under this section, except that section 14 of the Federal Advisory Committee Act shall not apply to the Advisory Committee established under this section.

Sec. 6008. DOT Data Needs.
(105 Stat. 2175)

(a) Study.-Not later than 1 year after the date of the establishment of the Bureau of Transportation Statistics, the Secretary shall enter into an agreement with the National Academy of Sciences to conduct a study on the adequacy of data collection procedures and capabilities of the Department of Transportation.

(b) Consultation.-The Secretary shall enter into the agreement under subsection (a) in consultation with the Director of the Bureau of Transportation Statistics.

(c) Contents.-The study under subsection (a) shall include an evaluation of the Department of Transportation's data collection resources, needs, and requirements and an assessment and evaluation of the systems, capabilities, and procedures established by the Department to meet such needs and requirements, including the following:

   (1) Data collection procedures and capabilities.
   (2) Data analysis procedures and capabilities.
   (3) Ability of data bases to integrate with one another.
   (4) Computer hardware and software capabilities.
   (5) Information management systems, including the ability of information management systems to integrate with one another.
   (6) Availability and training of the personnel of the Department.
   (7) Budgetary needs and resources of the Department for data collection.

(d) Report.-Not later than 18 months after the date of the agreement under subsection (a), the National Academy of Sciences shall transmit to Congress a report on the results of the study under this section, including recommendations for improving the Department of Transportation's data collection systems, capabilities, procedures, and analytical hardware and software and recommendations for improving the Department's management information systems.

Sec. 6013. State Level of Effort.
(105 Stat. 2181)

(a) Study.-Not later than 3 months after the date of the enactment of this Act, the Secretary and the Director of the Bureau of Transportation Statistics shall begin a comprehensive study of the most appropriate and accurate methods of calculating State level of effort in funding surface transportation programs.

(b) Contents.-The study under subsection (a) shall include collection of data relating to State and local revenues collected and spent on surface transportation programs. Such revenues include income from fuel taxes, toll revenues (including bridge, tunnel, and ferry tolls), sales taxes, general fund appropriations, property taxes, bonds, administrative fees, taxes on commercial vehicles, and such other State and local revenue sources as the Director of the Bureau considers appropriate.

(c) Report.-Not later than 9 months after the date of the enactment of this Act, the Secretary and the Director of the Bureau shall transmit to the Committee on Environment and Public Works of the Senate and the Committee on Public Works and Transportation of the House of Representatives a report on the results of the study under this section, including recommendations on the most appropriate measure of State level of effort in funding surface transportation programs and comprehensive data, by State, on revenue sources and amounts collected by States and local governments and devoted to surface transportation programs.

Sec. 1098. Allocation Formula Study.
(105 Stat. 2025)

(a) The General Accounting Office in conjunction with the Bureau of Transportation Statistics created pursuant to title VI of this Act, shall conduct a thorough study and recommend to the Congress within 2 years after the date of the enactment of this Act a fair and equitable apportionment formula for the allocation of Federal-aid highway funds that best directs highway funds to the places of greatest need for highway maintenance and enhancement based on the extent of these highway systems, their present use, and increases in their use.

(b) The results of this study shall be presented to the Senate Committee on Environment and Public Works and the House Committee on Public Works and Transportation on or before January 1, 1994, and shall be considered by these committees as they reauthorize the surface transportation program in 1996.

SEC. 5002. Duties of Secretary; Office of Intermodalism
(105 Stat. 2158)
. . .

(c) Office of Intermodalism.-

(1) Establishment.-The Secretary shall establish within the Office of the Secretary an Office of Intermodalism.

. . .

(4) Intermodal transportation data base.-The Director shall develop, maintain, and disseminate intermodal transportation data through the Bureau of Transportation Statistics. The Director shall coordinate the collection of data for the data base with the States and metropolitan planning organizations. The data base shall include-

   (A) information on the volume of goods and number of people carried in intermodal transportation by relevant classification;
   (B) information on patterns of movement of goods and people carried in intermodal transportation by relevant classification in terms of origin and destination; and
   (C) information on public and private investment in intermodal transportation facilities and services.

The Director shall make information from the data base available to the public.

APPENDIX
B

Selected Statistical Agencies and Programs

MAJOR FEDERAL STATISTICAL AGENCIES

Below are brief descriptions of the origins of major federal statistical agencies, in order from the oldest to the newest agency. Sources are Duncan and Shelton (1978) and Norwood (1995). Table B-1 shows fiscal 1997 budgets for each agency.

National Agricultural Statistics Service (NASS), U.S. Department of Agriculture

Patent Office began collecting agricultural statistics in 1840; statistical research and analysis provided for in the Department of Agriculture in 1862; independent statistical agency created in the Department of Agriculture in 1961.

Statistics of Income (SOI) Program, U.S. Department of the Treasury

Statistical Bureau created by law in 1866; made part of the new Department of Commerce and Labor in 1903; made part of the Department of the Treasury in 1913; merged with Compliance Research in 1996.

National Center for Education Statistics (NCES), U.S. Department of Education

Statistics on condition and progress of education established by law 1867; became part of the new Department of Health, Education, and Welfare in 1953; made part of the new Department of Education in 1979 with broadened role.

TABLE B-1 Fiscal 1997 Budget Amounts (Estimated) for Major Federal Statistical Agencies

Agency	Fiscal 1997 Budget (millions of dollars)
Bureau of the Census	
Current programs	145.0
Periodic programs (censuses)	210.5
Bureau of Economic Analysis	40.9
Bureau of Justice Statistics	21.4
Bureau of Labor Statistics	360.8
Bureau of Transportation Statistics	24.8
Energy Information Administration	70.9
National Agricultural Statistics Service	100.2
National Center for Education Statistics	82.6
National Center for Health Statistics	86.0
Statistics of Income, Internal Revenue Service	24.7

NOTE: Funding levels shown for NCES and BJS do not include salaries and expenses from other departmental sources.

SOURCE: Council of Professional Associations on Federal Statistics (1997:8).

Bureau of Labor Statistics (BLS), U.S. Department of Labor

Created as Bureau of Labor in Department of the Interior by law in 1884; became an independent agency that acted as a department of labor without executive rank; became a bureau in the new Department of Commerce and Labor in 1903; became part of the new Department of Labor in 1913.

Bureau of the Census, U.S. Department of Commerce

Decennial census required by Constitution beginning in 1790; became a permanent bureau with an expanded mission in 1903 in the new Department of Commerce and Labor; made part of the new Department of Commerce in 1913.

National Center for Health Statistics (NCHS), U.S. Department of Health and Human Services

Health data a concern of Public Health Service as early as 1912; made part of the new Department of Health, Education, and Welfare in 1953; made part of the new Department of Health and Human Services in 1979.

Bureau of Economic Analysis (BEA), U.S. Department of Commerce

Created as the Office of Business Economics in the Department of Commerce in 1953.

Energy Information Administration (EIA), U.S. Department of Energy

Created by law in 1977 in the new Department of Energy, which consolidated energy-related activities.

Bureau of Justice Statistics (BJS), U.S. Department of Justice

The direct antecedent of BJS was the Law Enforcement Assistance Administration; BJS created by the Justice System Improvement Act of 1979.

Bureau of Transportation Statistics (BTS), U.S. Department of Transportation

Created by the Intermodal Surface Transportation Efficiency Act of 1991.

MODAL ADMINISTRATIONS AND STATISTICAL UNITS IN USDOT

Below is information about the modal administrations in USDOT (in alphabetical order) on total fiscal 1997 appropriated budget and the estimated 1997 budget and 1996 number of full-time-equivalent (FTE) staff for major statistical units within each modal administration. Most statistical units have assistance from contractor staff who supplement their own staff; for example, BTS has an estimated 52 contract employees, not including Census Bureau staff who work on the Commodity Flow Survey and the American Travel Survey; the Safety Data Services Division of the Federal Aviation Administration has an estimated 28 contract employees; and the National Center for Statistics and Analysis of the National Highway Traffic Safety Administration has an estimated 12 contract employees. Budget information (obligations) for the modal administrations is from Executive Office of the President (1997a); information on programs, budget, and staffing of major statistical units is from interviews with agency staff in fall 1996.

Bureau of Transportation Statistics (BTS)

Total FY 1997 Budget: $25 million
1996 FTE Staffing: 37 federal employees

Federal Aviation Administration (FAA)

Total FY 1997 Budget: $8.6 billion
Major Statistical Unit:
Safety Data Services Division; includes National Aviation Safety Data Analysis Center, which publishes quarterly indicators; 12 federal employees; FY 1997 budget of $4 million.

Federal Highway Administration (FHWA)

Total FY 1997 Budget: $20.6 billion
Major Statistical Unit:
Office of Highway Information Management; operates Highway Performance Monitoring System and General Highway Statistics Program; 35 federal employees; FY 1997 budget of $33 million.

Federal Railroad Administration (FRA)

Total FY 1997 Budget: $1.2 billion
Major Statistical Programs:
FY 1997 budget of $1.5 million; no separate statistical units.

Federal Transit Administration (FTA)

Total FY 1997 Budget: $5.5 billion
Major Statistical Unit:
Part of Office of Program Guidance and Support operates the National Transit Data Base; 4 federal employees; FY 1997 budget of $2 million.

Maritime Administration (MARAD)

Total FY 1997 Budget: $284 million
Major Statistical Unit:
Office of Statistical and Economic Analysis; 20 federal employees; FY 1997 budget of $1.6 million.

National Highway Traffic Safety Administration (NHTSA)

Total FY 1997 Budget: $300 million
Major Statistical Unit:
National Center for Statistics and Analysis; operates the Fatal Accident Reporting System and National Accident Sampling System; 40 federal employees; FY 1997 budget of $27 million.

Research and Special Programs Administration (RSPA)

Total FY 1997 Budget: $271 million
Major Statistical Programs:
FY 1997 budget of $3 million; no separate statistical units.

St. Lawrence Seaway Development Corporation (SLSDC)

Total FY 1997 Budget: $12 million; limited statistical activities.

U.S. Coast Guard (USCG)

Total FY 1997 Budget: $3.9 billion; limited statistical activities.

APPENDIX
C

Principles and Practices for a Federal Statistical Agency: How BTS Compares

The Committee on National Statistics (CNSTAT) in *Principles and Practices for a Federal Statistical Agency* (NRC, 1992b) listed a series of issues that it considered important for the proper functioning of a statistical agency. The following list includes a series of points culled from that report with a review of their application to the Bureau of Transportation Statistics (BTS). The boldface type in this appendix is based on excerpts from the text in the CNSTAT publication. Each excerpt of a principle or practice is followed, in regular type, by a brief evaluation of its application to BTS. The excerpts are sometimes shortened, rephrased, or grouped together for clarity.

A. A federal statistical agency is a unit of the federal government whose principal function is the compilation and analysis of data and the dissemination of information for statistical purposes. The unit must be generally recognized as a distinct entity. It may be located within a cabinet department or an independent agency.

The mission for BTS—to compile, analyze, and disseminate information—was established by the 1991 ISTEA legislation. BTS has begun two major multimodal surveys, produced several analytical reports, and developed computerized approaches to dissemination of data on transportation. BTS is a separate agency within the U.S. Department of Transportation (USDOT) with a director reporting directly to the secretary of transportation.

B. A federal statistical agency must be in a position to provide information relevant to issues of public policy.

BTS provides some information to support transportation policy making, and the BTS director provides information analysis for the secretary of transportation.

However, BTS has not yet developed a long-range plan for data needed for transportation policy, nor has it developed a set of indicators of the transportation system and its problems. BTS has taken steps to develop needed new data. It has not yet played a vigorous role in the coordination of transportation data collection within its own department or within the federal statistical community.

C. A federal statistical agency must have a relationship of mutual respect and trust with those who use its data and information.

BTS provides services to users of transportation data, especially by bringing together data from many sources and putting them into more accessible form. However, as a statistical agency, BTS does not yet have a well-developed program to inform its users about the quality of the data it makes accessible to them.

D. A federal statistical agency must have a relationship of mutual respect and trust with respondents who provide data and with all data subjects whose information it obtains.

The two major surveys begun by BTS—the American Travel Survey and the Commodity Flow Survey—are conducted for it by the Bureau of the Census. The surveys are carried out in accordance with Census Bureau procedures for treating respondents and on maintaining the confidentiality of the data collected. The 1991 ISTEA legislation provides legislative authority for the protection of the confidentiality of data collected by BTS. Recently, however, the compilation and publication of airline and motor carrier information was transferred to BTS; these programs require publication of the data collected identified by name of the responding organization. The airline data are also used for some regulatory purposes.

E. An agency's mission should include responsibility for assessing needs for information and determining sources of data, measurement methods, and efficient methods of collection and ensuring the public availability of needed data, including, if necessary, the establishment of a data collection program.

BTS has moved forward rapidly to contract with the Census Bureau to implement the Commodity Flow Survey and the American Travel Survey, which provide intermodal data that have not been available for over 15 years. BTS has also worked with the American Association of State Highway and Transportation Officials, the American Association of Metropolitan Planning Organizations, and the Transportation Research Board to help states and localities assess data needs and to understand the data that are already available. In general, BTS has thus far focused more attention on the dissemination of data that are available than on the identification of data gaps and programs to fill them.

F. A statistical agency must have independence mandated in organic legislation or encouraged by organizational structure. In essence, a statistical agency must be distinct from the enforcement and policy-making activities carried out by the department in which the agency is located. The independence of the agency head must be understood. The statistical agency must have broad authority over scope, content, and frequency of data collected, compiled, or published.

The director of BTS is appointed by the president with the consent of the Senate. The director has a fixed 4-year term of office and does not serve at the pleasure of the president. BTS functions as a separate agency within USDOT. BTS has broad authority over its publications and other programs. It does not have authority over the statistical programs located in other parts of the department. However, it is clear that the 1991 ISTEA envisioned BTS as providing leadership throughout USDOT and the entire statistical system on transportation issues. BTS has not yet made an attempt to establish guidelines for data quality and definitions for use throughout USDOT.

G. A statistical agency should have primary authority for selection and promotion of professional staff.

Although, like other executive branch agencies, BTS is affected by general staffing rules and limitations, BTS controls the selection and promotion of its employees. With the exception of the director who is a presidential appointee, all BTS personnel are career civil servants.

H. It is important that the agency head be recognized as professionally qualified and have direct access to the secretary of the department in which the agency is located.

The 1991 ISTEA requires that the director of BTS be professionally qualified for the position. Since BTS has the status of a USDOT modal administration, its director has direct access to the secretary of transportation. The first director, T.R. Lakshmanan, is well regarded in transportation and academic circles and provides objective, apolitical advice to the secretary of transportation.

I. The agency should be recognized by policy officials outside the statistical agency for its authority to release statistical information without prior clearance.

BTS has followed a policy of releasing data without prior clearance from USDOT officials.

J. The statistical agency head and qualified staff should be able to speak on the agency's statistical program before Congress.

BTS has this authority, and its director has testified before the Congress on transportation statistics. BTS is, of course, subject to the same rules as for all executive branch agencies of having prior clearance by the Office of Management and Budget of prepared congressional testimony.

K. There should be a clear distinction between the release of statistical information and the policy interpretations of such statements by the secretary of the department, the president, or others. It is also useful for the agency to adhere to predetermined schedules in public release of important economic or other indicator data to prevent manipulation of release dates for political purposes.

BTS has a clear understanding of the need to maintain the objectivity of its data and has endeavored to keep the distinction between statistical information and policy prescription. The director has paid a great deal of attention to the separation between objective data and political policy and has made sure that the BTS does not involve itself in policy determination. BTS does not yet have a program of key transportation indicators released on a regular basis.

L. To maintain credibility and a relationship of respect and trust with data providers and users, an agency must observe fair information practices, including maintaining the confidentiality of individual responses and seeking the cooperation of data providers and users through consultation.

BTS has legislation to protect the confidentiality of data provided by individuals and businesses and, in the data collected by the Bureau of the Census, uses Census Bureau rules on this issue. As indicated above, the nature of airline and motor carrier information identified by respondent poses special problems and is inconsistent with the principle of statistical confidentiality necessary to maintain survey response rates and a statistical agency's reputation for objectivity.

BTS has successfully developed several mechanisms for obtaining user input on data products, including a customer survey and e-mail response capability on its World Wide Web site. It has worked with the states and with other users of transportation data. BTS also has an advisory committee that meets twice a year to review its program as a whole. BTS has no systematic means of input on data concepts, priorities, and methods.

M. A statistical agency should exercise care to make its data equally accessible to all potential users.

BTS has made it a priority to provide access to its own data and transportation data from other sources to the widest possible audience through the World Wide Web and other media. BTS treats all users on an equal basis.

N. An agency should fully describe its data and comment on their relevance to specific major uses. It should describe the methods used, the assumptions made, the limitations of the data, the manners by which data linkages are made, and the results of research on the methods and data.

The American Travel Survey and the Commodity Flow Survey, collected for BTS by the Bureau of the Census, follow Census Bureau standards for publication of sampling error and information on survey design. The analyses included in the *Transportation Statistics Annual Reports* published by BTS refer to the data on which the analysis is based in ways that may be useful to readers. Otherwise, BTS has emphasized gathering data from many sources and making them available in machine-readable format. The agency has devoted little attention to documentation of quality and limitations of data on its web site. BTS has few staff devoted to methodological research.

O. A statistical agency should develop strong staff expertise in the disciplines relevant to its mission as well as in the theory and practice of statistics. Measures of uncertainty should be provided to users, and statistical standards should be published to guide professionals in the agency as well as external users.

Although BTS has staff experienced in analysis of transportation data, it has relatively few people on its staff with statistical expertise. As a consequence, except for the two surveys mentioned above, BTS has done little with regard to evaluation and documentation of the data it publishes and makes available on the Internet. Except for the American Travel Survey and the Commodity Flow Survey, BTS provides only limited information on sources of error for the data in its own publications. BTS has done little thus far to develop standards of good statistical practice for its own use or for use by other units of USDOT.

P. An agency should develop a strong and continuous relationship with appropriate professional statistical organizations. It should have a research program that is integral to its activities.

BTS has a series of regular technical seminars for its own staff that are also open to others in USDOT. The seminars provide an opportunity for discussion of scientific research on a continuing basis with outside researchers in the field of transportation. In addition, BTS has sponsored conferences with papers prepared by scholars in this country and abroad on issues important for an understanding of transportation problems. BTS has initiated a new journal that will include peer-reviewed papers on topics in transportation, including research methods. BTS has an advisory committee made up of people knowledgeable about transportation issues and statistical policy. BTS has not yet developed strong relationships with such associations as the American Statistical Association, nor has it conducted methodological research.

Q. A statistical agency must recruit and retain a professional staff of high caliber—both statisticians and analysts in fields relevant to its mission. Personnel policies should encourage staff to maintain and extend their capabilities through appropriate professional activities.

BTS has a capable staff knowledgeable in the field of transportation. The agency augments this staff when necessary through contracting arrangements to obtain the services of people with needed skills. The agency is young and still quite small, however, and has thus far very few on its staff with strong statistical expertise. As indicated above, its seminar program and new journal should provide a means for intellectual discussion and professional interaction and development for its staff.

R. An agency should release information identified with a specific organization or entity for a nonstatistical purpose only when such release would not conflict with the agency's mission.

The Office of Airline Information within BTS releases identifiable information in accordance with the *Code of Federal Regulations*. In addition, the Motor Carrier Statistics Program, recently transferred to BTS, identifies individual carriers. Both sets of data products may be used for nonstatistical purposes. The remainder of the BTS activities are for statistical purposes only.

S. Data sharing and statistical uses of administrative records make a

statistical agency more effective as well as efficient. An effective statistical agency promotes data linkages.

BTS has initiated work with the Bureau of Economic Analysis to develop a transportation satellite account as part of the National Income and Product Accounts. BTS has a good record of working with agencies, both inside and outside USDOT, to provide useful transportation data, but it has not yet promoted data linkages with the surveys of other agencies in the federal statistical system.

T. Federal statistical agencies should cooperate with state and local agencies in the provision of data for subnational areas. Agencies should cooperate also with foreign and international statistical agencies to exchange information, on both data and methods, and to develop common classifications and procedures.

Several of the USDOT modal administrations have long-established programs of federal-state-local data collection. BTS has made an effort to find ways to assist states and localities to obtain and use data more effectively. BTS has also begun development of relationships with foreign and international agencies.

APPENDIX
D

Improving *National Transportation Statistics:* Airline Safety as a Case Study

The annual *National Transportation Statistics (NTS)* report published by BTS is a reference publication that compiles a large number of transportation data series in a single, regularly updated volume. Each year's report contains a profile of financial, operating, and safety characteristics of each transportation mode—highway, rail, air, etc. Each year's compendium also has sections on such topics as safety, with tables and graphs for all of the transportation modes. Most tables and graphs provide time series of data in 5-year or 10-year intervals for the past 2 or 3 decades, with annual data for the most recent 3 to 4 years. (As in the *Statistical Abstract of the United States,* which annually provides a large number of tables on a broad range of subjects, there is no analytical commentary in the *NTS* reports.)

Although bringing together a large amount of data in a convenient form, the usefulness of the *NTS* reports as reference documents is affected by the scarcity of explanatory notes, including those that would describe important changes in definitions of variables across time (see Chapter 3). Also lacking are explanations that would help users understand the extent to which it is appropriate to compare data series on particular topics across transportation modes. Finally, the graphs and charts that are included are not always helpful or appropriate. (The most recent *1997 NTS* report includes more tables than previous reports and eliminates all charts and graphs.)

We reviewed the tables and graphs on airline safety from the *1996 NTS* as a case study to identify some of the problems with the *NTS* reports and ways in which BTS could improve them, topic by topic, over the next few years. The publication is valuable; our goal in the case study was to identify areas for improvement. The *1997 NTS*—which became available to the panel only after its work was finished—reflects improvements that anticipate many of our comments; further improvements can be made, particularly in providing more detailed explanatory notes. (BTS is completing a review of the *1997 NTS* to this end.) Below we present an abbreviated version of our case study from the *1996 NTS*.

REVIEW OF *1996 NTS* AIRLINE SAFETY STATISTICS: CONCLUSIONS

The commentary below addresses selected tables and graphs on airline safety from the *1996 NTS*, with suggestions for changes that could help the user make appropriate comparisons over time and across transportation modes or categories of a mode. For airlines, categories include major U.S. air carriers, commuter carriers, on-demand air taxis, and general aviation. The commentary makes a number of main points:

- There are no graphs of accident and fatality rates across airline categories that provide data on a comparable basis.
- There are no tables or graphs that break down the components of underlying trends (e.g., growth in aircraft passenger-miles as a function of the number of flights, distance per flight, and number of passengers per flight) or that draw out their implications for safety trends.
- Tables on the same topic do not always contain comparable data, and there is inadequate warning to users when this occurs.
- Graphs are provided for raw counts (e.g., numbers of accidents or fatalities, sometimes with different scales), when such numbers are likely misleading in the absence of information about exposure (i.e., when the counts are not converted to rates by the use of appropriate denominators—a point that is made in the BTS *Transportation Statistics Annual Reports*).
- Although sources are cited, there is no information provided about the underlying data systems or the quality of the data.

REVIEW OF *1996 NTS* AIRLINE SAFETY STATISTICS: COMMENTARY

Air Carrier Profile

The profile section provides numbers of accidents, fatal accidents, and fatalities for scheduled and nonscheduled airlines operating under 14 CFR 121 and for scheduled commuter airlines and nonscheduled on-demand air taxis operating under 14 CFR 35. (CFR, which stands for the *Code of Federal Regulations*, is nowhere defined.) The profile also provides performance data on aircraft revenue-miles, aircraft revenue-hours, revenue passenger-miles, and revenue passenger emplanements, which could serve as denominators with which to compute accident and fatality rates. However, the performance data are provided for different categories of airlines than are the safety data (e.g., majors, nationals, large regionals), and there is no explanation of how the categories in the performance and safety portions of the profile relate, or if indeed they can be related.

Safety Section

Table 28—Fatalities, Injuries, and Accidents by Mode

The data in Table 28 for U.S. air carriers, commuter air carriers, and on-demand air taxis match the data in the profile; however, the Table 28 definition of air carriers is "large" carriers operating under 14 CFR 121, which implies something different from all carriers operating under that set of regulations. Citations are provided in a separate section; no information is provided about any of the major data sources or how they might compare across transportation modes.

Figure 9—Fatalities by Transportation Mode, 1960-1994

Figure 9 provides two bar graphs, each showing trends for 4 transportation modes. Two modes are omitted entirely: motor vehicle traffic and rail-highway grade crossings. The two graphs differ in scale on the vertical axis, which means that the reader may incorrectly infer that waterborne transport in the 1970s (bottom graph) was considerably more hazardous than, say, general aviation in the same time period (top graph). The use of the same scale on the horizontal axis for single years from 1990 to 1994 as for 5-year intervals from 1960 to 1990 in this and other graphs may mislead the reader about time trends.

A more useful presentation could be to have a set of line graphs for all of the modes with appropriate time intervals and a common vertical scale, with a break in the scale at the top for motor vehicle traffic. However, there is a real question as to the value of graphing the number of fatalities (or accidents) at all, given differences in the exposure of the population to risk.

Table 30 and Figure 11—U.S. Air Carrier Accident and Fatal Accident Rates per Million Aircraft Miles Flown

The data on millions of aircraft miles flown in Table 30 cannot be related to the profile.

Figure 11 provides two graphs, one on trends in millions of aircraft-miles flown and another on accident and fatal accident rates per million miles flown. It could be useful to provide text explaining that changes in aircraft-miles flown are a function of changes in the number of takeoffs (flights) and changes in the distance flown per flight. If data exist on these components, it could be useful to show them together with the trends in total aircraft-miles flown. It could also be useful to show accident and fatal accident rates per 100,000 takeoffs, as in Table 36 for commuter air carriers, and to explain briefly when one denominator might be more appropriate to use than another.

Table 31 and Figure 12—U.S. Air Carrier Passenger Fatality Rates per 100 Million Passenger-Miles

The data on fatalities in Table 31 are for scheduled service only and so do not match the data in Table 28. The data on fatalities can be matched to the data in the profile, but not so the data on revenue passenger-miles.

Figure 12 contains three graphs—for trends in revenue passenger-miles, number of fatalities, and the passenger fatality rate. The usefulness of the graph on number of fatalities, given that the vertical scale is so greatly different from that of the other graphs and that there is no measure of risk exposure, is open to question (the data are available in Table 31). Text could usefully be added to explain that trends in passenger-miles are a function of trends in three factors: number of takeoffs (flights), distance per flight, and number of passengers per flight. If data exist on these components, it could be useful to show them, as well as to show fatality rates for other denominators (e.g., 100,000 passengers) and briefly explain when one denominator might be more appropriate to use than another.

Table 32 and Figure 13—U.S. Air Carrier Accidents and Serious Injuries

Figure 13 graphs numbers of accidents and serious injuries, which do not appear to be useful to show in graphical form, given the absence of denominators.

Table 36—Commuter Air Carrier Accidents, Fatalities, Injuries, and Accident Rates

Table 36 provides accident and fatal accident rates per million aircraft-miles flown and per 100,000 departures. No rates are given for fatalities, and no graphs are shown. It could be useful to show graphs that compare accident and fatality rates for U.S. air carriers and commuter air carriers on a common basis, if this is possible.

Table 37—On-Demand Air Taxi Accidents, Fatalities, Injuries, and Accident Rates

Table 37 provides accident and fatal accident rates per 100,000 aircraft hours flown. No rates are given for fatalities, and no graphs are shown. It would be useful if accident and fatality rates could be compared for on-demand air taxis and other aviation modes (e.g., commuter airlines) on a common basis. If no data exist for this purpose, it would be useful to point out this fact.

Table 38 and Figure 16—General Aviation Accidents, Fatalities, Serious Injuries, and Fatal Accidents; Table 39 and Figure 17—General Aviation Fatality and Accident Rates per 100,000 Aircraft-Hours

Figure 16 provides numbers but not rates; its usefulness is open to question. Table 39 and Figure 17 provide rates for one denominator—aircraft-hours flown. Presumably other rates could be calculated on the basis of the information in the general aviation profile, which provides information on vehicle-miles and passenger-miles as well as aircraft-hours flown. However, the profile estimates of hours flown do not always agree with the estimates in Table 39. If possible, it would be useful to provide graphs that compare accident and fatality rates for general aviation with the other aviation modes.

APPENDIX E

Descriptions of CD-ROM Products on the BTS Web Site

The BTS World Wide Web site, in addition to making some data sets directly accessible, describes other data sets that are available on CD-ROM. To facilitate users' ability to locate high-quality, relevant data, it is important that the brief descriptions of CD-ROM products follow a standardized format that is as informative as possible. However, the descriptions that BTS provides for its CD-ROM products in the "Products" section of its web site vary in their content, usefulness, and, in some instances, compatibility with information for the same product from other sections of the web site.

This appendix reproduces descriptions of selected BTS CD-ROM products from the BTS web site, pointing out examples of better and worse practice. A useful format may be one that organizes the specific items of information that are provided for each entry in the BTS *Directory of Transportation Data Sources* (see Chapter 3) under the general headings that are used in the web site descriptions of many of the data sets: What is it? What's in it? How can I use it? and Product format. Also, it is important to provide a contact name for additional information.

COMMENTARY ON CD-ROM DESCRIPTIONS

1990 Census Transportation Planning Package (CTPP)—Statewide Element

The description of the CTPP—Statewide Element CD-ROM has information under the following headings: What is it? What's in it? How can I use it? and Product format (see Figure E-1). The information provided on content is limited

131

APPENDIX E

SERVICES & PRODUCTS ▶ PRODUCTS

1990 Census Transportation Planning Package - Statewide Element

What is it?

The *1990 Census Transportation Planning Package* (CTPP)CD-ROM is a set of special tabulations of 1990 census data tailored to meet the data needs of transportation planners. Tabulations also contain a wealth of general interest information on the work force by place of work. The 1990 CTPP is a continuation of the program established for the 1970 census and continued for the 1980 census in the same general format.

What's in it?

Statewide tabulations on the following:

- **Part A**...characteristics of persons, workers, and housing units by county, place of 2,500 or more (city, town, village, etc.), and county subdivision (where requested) of residence.
- **Part B**...characteristics of workers by county, place of 2,500 or more, and county subdivision (where requested) of work.
- **Part C**...characteristics of workers in journey-to-work flows between counties, places of 2,500 or more, and county subdivision (where requested) of residence and counties and   places of 2,500 or more of work.

How can I use it?

- CTPP may be accessed using TransVU software which is provided separately with the CD-ROM. TransVU is a Windows application that provides both map and tabular views of CTPP data and simplifies extraction of C TPP tables into dBase, Lotus, and comma delimited or fixed format ascii text files. Users can select tables by summary level, by topic, by universe, or geographic location.
- Raw data may also be accessed directly by users with their own data manipulation software.

PRODUCT FORMAT: 1990 Census Transportation Planning Package is available on a set of 12 CD-ROMs for the entire United States from the Bureau of Transportation Statistics. Customers are asked to specify data for the states they require. TransVU software is provided on diskette with the CTPP CD-ROM.

[Alphabetical Listing] [Subject Listing] [Media Listing] [Mode Listing]

[BTS Products Page] [BTS Services] [Order Form]

Feedback? Questions? comments@bts.gov

FIGURE E-1 Description of the CTPP—Statewide Element CD-ROM.

(e.g., "characteristics of persons, workers, and housing units"). There is no mention that the data are from a sample (the census long form), nor that the data on place of work involve geocoding address information provided by census respondents that may have significant levels of error. No contact name for additional information is provided.

1990 Census Transportation Planning Package (CTPP)—Urban

The description of the CTPP—Urban Element CD-ROM (not shown) follows the same format as the description of the companion Statewide CD-ROM (see Figure E-1). It is fairly informative with regard to content. However, there is no mention that the data are from a sample, nor of the average population size of the areas—traffic zones and census tracts—for which data are provided on this CD-ROM. There is no contact name for additional information.

Commodity Flow Survey (CFS), 1993

The description of the CFS that was on the BTS web site until late March 1997 followed the same format as the entries in the *Directory of Transportation Data Sources* (see Chapter 3). It had the following headings: Mode; Abstract (including an overview of the survey design and content); Source of data; Attributes (geographic coverage, time span of data, first developed, update frequency, number of records, file size, file format, media); Significant features and/or limitations; Corresponding printed source; Sponsoring organization; Performing organization; Availability; Contact for additional information. The description was quite complete, although the addition of information on response rates and publications would have made it more useful. The description was subsequently revised to use the following headings: What is it? What's in it? How can I use it? and Product Format. In the revision (not shown), some useful information was not retained, although other useful information was added.

Nationwide Personal Transportation Survey (NPTS), 1983 and 1990

The description of the Nationwide Personal Transportation Survey has information under the headings: What is it? What's in it? How can I use it? and Product format (see Figure E-2). The description is reasonably informative about content. However, it does not provide information about sample size or whether there is any identification of subnational geographic areas, such as regions. (The NPTS sample size of about 22,000 households is too small to provide much geographic detail.) No contact name for additional information is provided.

Nationwide Personal Transportation Survey 1983 and 1990

What Is It?

The *Nationwide Personal Transportation Survey* (NPTS) compiles national data on the nature and characteristics of personal travel by all modes of transportation. Information from a national household sample was collected about all trips taken during a designated 24-hour period (travel day). Additional details were collected for trips of 75 miles or further (one-way) that were taken during the preceding 14-day period (travel period) including the 24-hour travel day. NPTS data, which are collected by the U.S. Department of Transportation's Federal Highway Administration, are available for 1983 and 1990 on this product.

What's in it?

- Demographic characteristics of persons and households include such topics as relationship of household members, educational levels through graduate or professional school, income categories, etc.;
- ❏ Household vehicle availability and use;
- ❏ Annual miles per licensed driver;
- ❏ Household travel rates;
- ❏ Day-of-week and time-of-day travel;
- ❏ Vehicle occupancy; and
- ❏ Home-to-work trips.

How can I use it?

- To track, over time, both personal travel and the characteristics related to that travel for the entire nation.
- The *Nationwide Personal Transportation Survey* CD-ROM contains the Statistical Export and Tabulation System (SETS) software program, developed by the National Center for Health Statistics, that allows use rs to access documentation and data stored on disks or on a CD-ROM.
- SETS allows users to browse through and print documentation and data; build a table and query data; and, export documentation and data in dBase compatible (.DBF) format or SAS, SPSS, EPI Info, and BMDP formats.

PRODUCT FORMAT: *Nationwide Personal Transportation Survey* (NPTS)is available on CD-ROM from the Bureau of Transportation Statistics.

[Alphabetical Listing] [Subject Listing] [Media Listing] [Mode Listing]

[BTS Products Page] [BTS Services] [Order Form]

Feedback? Questions? comments@bts.gov

FIGURE E-2   Description of the Nationwide Personal Transportation Survey 1983 and 1990.

Traffic Safety Data CD-ROM

The description of the Traffic Safety CD-ROM, which contains data from the Fatal Accident Reporting System (FARS) and General Estimates System (GES) of the National Highway Traffic Safety Administration (NHTSA), is only a brief paragraph (see Figure E-3). It informs the user that the CD-ROM includes an analytic reference guide that describes the comparability of the data over the evolution of the NHTSA programs. (However, none of the available documentation for the traffic safety data describes the collection methodology in detail or possible sources of errors.) No contact name for additional information is provided.

Previously, a somewhat longer description of the Traffic Safety Data CD-ROM was available that provided information under the following headings: What is it? What's in it? How can I use it? and Product format. This description is no longer linked to the "Products" section of the BTS web site; however, it appears when one follows the pathway through the National Transportation Data Archive section of the site to the entry for the Fatal Accident Reporting System Database, which contains a link to the CD-ROM description.

Traffic Safety Data CD-ROM

Traffic Safety Data CD-ROM contains the *Fatal Accident Reporting System (FARS) 1975-1994* and *General Estimates System (GES) 1988-1994* in ASCII format. These data are collected by the U.S. Department of Transportation's National Highway Traffic Safety Administration (NHTSA). Also included on this cd-rom are the *FARS Analytic Reference Guide 1975-1995*, a detailed reference source describing the comparability of data variables over the course of the survey's evolution. In addition, NHTSA's *Traffic Safety Report 1994* and *Traffic Safety Fact Sheets* are included on this CD-ROM and may be browsed using the on-disc Folio software.

[Alphabetical Listing] [Subject Listing] [Media Listing] [Mode Listing]

[BTS Products Page] [BTS Services] [Order Form]

Feedback? Questions? comments@bts.gov

FIGURE E-3   Description of the Traffic Safety Data CD-ROM.

What is it?

The Bureau of Transportation Statistics's Transborder Surface Freight Dataset, available since April 1993, contains freight flow data by commodity type and by surface mode of transportation (rail, truck, pipeline or mail) for U.S. exports to and imports from Canada and Mexico. The data are processed and summarized for BTS by the U.S. Census Bureau on a monthly basis.

What's in it?

The Transborder Surface Freight dataset provides previously unpublished surface transportation data (other than air or maritime vessel) for U.S. import and export trade with or through Canada and Mexico. The dataset includes two sets of tables; one is commodity based while the other provides geographic detail.

The source data for import and exports are the administrative trade records required by the U.S. Departments of Commerce and Treasury. An increasing amount of import and export statistical information is now being captured electronically. For imports from Canada and Mexico, approximately 95 percent of the value of those imports is collected electronically via the Automated Broker Interface (ABI). For exports to Mexico, approximately 55 percent are collected through the Automated Export Reporting Program (AERP) where data are filed directly with the U.S. Census Bureau while the remainder are collected from paper export documents (Shippers' Export Declarations (SEDs)) that are filed with the U.S. Customs Service and processed by the U.S. Census Bureau. Exports to Canada are obtained through the U.S./Canada Data Exchange, under which the U.S. obtains the data Canada uses for its imports from the U.S.

How can I use it?

The Transborder Surface Freight Dataset is being used by a variety of organizations for a number of purposes, including the monitoring of freight flows and changes to these since the signing of the North American Free Trade Agreement (NAFTA) by the United States, Canada and Mexico in December 1993 and its entry into force on January 1, 1994. In addition, the dataset is being used by:

FIGURE E-4 Description of the Transborder Surface Freight Transportation Dataset.

- news organizations in reports;
- consultants in trade corridor studies;
- businesses in marketing plans and logistics studies;
- academic institutions in trade and transportation analyses;
- state and local government organizations for economic development studies and transportation and infrastructure planning purposes.

PRODUCT FORMAT: The Transborder Surface Freight Dataset is available at the Bureau of Transportation Statistics' Internet site.

[Alphabetical Listing] [Subject Listing] [Media Listing] [Mode Listing]

[BTS Products Page] [BTS Services] [Order Form]

Feedback? Questions? comments@bts.gov

FIGURE E-4   Continued

Transborder Surface Freight Data

The description of the Transborder Surface Freight Transportation data set, which contains information on quarterly shipments between the United States and Mexico and the United States and Canada from unpublished customs data processed by the Census Bureau, has information under the headings: What is it? What's in it? How can I use it? and Product format (see Figure E-4). The description of content is brief—for example, the user is not informed as to whether the data pertain to value, tonnage of shipments, or some other metric. "Product format" is listed, not as a CD-ROM, but as data that are directly accessible on the BTS web site. The data are in fact accessible through the National Transportation Data Archive section of the site, at which location they are searchable by state and commodity code. The data are also available on a CD-ROM, but the data set description that is linked to the "Products" section of the web site no longer mentions the CD-ROM product. (An earlier description advertised the availability of the CD-ROM but did not mention the direct availability of the data on the BTS web site.)

APPENDIX F
Integrating Data and Filling Gaps: The Case of Household Travel

Budget constraints make it difficult for statistical agencies to garner sufficient resources to launch new data collection programs that are responsive to changing policy concerns and at the same time maintain and improve needed data series from the past. One way to free up resources for new or modified data collection is to integrate two or more existing data systems into a more cost-effective combined system. Even when data integration does not result in net cost savings, it can still be useful to undertake if the combined data are relevant for a wider range of analyses. Sometimes full integration is not possible or sensible, but partial links among data systems, achieved through such means as the use of consistent definitions for key variables, can significantly enhance their analytical power. Finally, efforts to relate multiple data systems will often identify important gaps that none of them currently fills.

To develop examples of possibilities for linking and integrating transportation data sources that BTS might usefully explore with other relevant agencies, we reviewed surveys that provide data on household transportation. Information on household travel, taking account of all transportation modes, is critical for many important transportation policy concerns, including access, safety, direct costs to the household sector, and indirect costs in terms of energy use, environmental effects, and economic productivity.

The two most important national surveys of household transportation are the American Travel Survey (ATS) sponsored by BTS and the Nationwide Personal Transportation Survey (NPTS) sponsored by the Office of Highway Information Management (OHIM) in the Federal Highway Administration (FHWA). The decennial census long-form sample, the Consumer Expenditure Survey (CEX) of the Bureau of Labor Statistics (BLS), and the Residential Transportation Energy

Consumption Survey (RTECS) of the Energy Information Administration (EIA) also provide relevant data. (EIA recently discontinued RTECS because of budget reductions.)

We drew two main conclusions from this review. First, there appears to be an opportunity to develop a more cost-effective data collection system for household travel by integrating the ATS and the NPTS. Second, looking across all of the existing surveys, there appear to be important data gaps that should be filled.

INTEGRATING THE ATS AND THE NPTS

The NPTS, which is currently conducted on the same 5-year cycle as the ATS, is designed to provide data on daily household travel patterns. The sample includes about 22,000 households, who are asked about trips during a specified travel day. They are also asked about longer trips (75 or more miles) over the previous two weeks, but these data are not adequate for purposes of analysis given the short reference period and small sample size. The NPTS sample size also limits the geographic areas for which estimates can be published to the United States, urban areas as a whole, rural areas as a whole, and groups of cities categorized by population size. A few states and metropolitan planning organizations (MPOs) pay for additional samples for their areas. (Many states, MPOs, and localities also conduct their own travel surveys independently.)

The ATS, under its current design, includes a sample of 80,000 households, who are asked 4 times over the course of a year about trips of 75 or more miles during each 3-month reference period. The data provide a complete picture of long trips for the year, but no questions are asked about shorter trips. The large sample size of the ATS permits analysis of flows of people between states and large metropolitan areas.

An integrated design for the ATS and the NPTS could provide useful data for federal, state, and MPO analysis and planning purposes, including consistent estimates of daily and long-distance household travel patterns, in a more cost-effective manner than two separate surveys, neither of which provides a complete picture of household transportation. A possible design (discussed in Chapter 3 in the context of the ATS alone) would be to conduct an annual survey of a relatively small sample of households to provide national estimates, with the sample augmented periodically to provide estimates for states and large MPOs. Each year's combined survey would ask questions both about daily travel patterns and about longer trips. To make the integration of the ATS and NPTS questionnaires feasible and not unduly burdensome to respondents, the sample could be divided into three groups, with one group of households asked only about daily travel, another group asked only about longer trips, and a third group asked about all trips. (This type of design was in fact used for the Nationwide Personal Transportation Survey in 1972 and 1977.)

ADDRESSING GAPS IN HOUSEHOLD TRAVEL DATA

Considering all of the existing household surveys (ATS, NPTS, decennial census, CEX, and RTECS), there are gaps in the data they provide. One such gap is data on commuting. Each of the existing surveys offers data that are relevant to commuting patterns. The decennial census long-form sample makes it possible once every 10 years to map commuting flows among small geographic areas and (since 1980) to determine travel time to work. The NPTS provides updates at 5-year intervals of modes of commuting and distance and time to work, but the sample size permits only limited geographic analysis. The ATS has a larger sample but only covers commuting trips of 75 or more miles (one-way) and does not ask about commuting time. None of these sources provides direct estimates of commuting costs (or about the costs of non-work-related transportation).

The omission of cost information seems quite important, given the productivity implications of commuting time and the expenses incurred by workers. As discussed in Chapter 3, BTS made a deliberate decision to exclude cost data from the ATS on the grounds that households underreport transportation costs. It expects that the U.S. Travel Data Center will develop model-based estimates of long-distance trip costs on the basis of trip characteristics. However, direct survey reports of costs could be useful input to model-based estimates and for validation.

The RTECS asked about modes of commuting and obtained data that permit a rough calculation of the costs of commuting for people who drive. The CEX obtains detailed cost data on transportation for vehicles and trips and usual monthly expenses for public transportation used for work and other purposes. However, the CEX has no data on vehicle miles traveled to work or total vehicle miles, and hence there is no ready way to calculate commuting costs for workers who drive. In addition, there is no way to relate public transportation costs to distance or time traveled. Both the RTECS and CEX sample sizes are quite small, limiting geographic analysis.

In summary, it is not possible to obtain from these data sources a complete picture of commuting flows, times, distances, and costs. The lack of complete data on commuting is an example of a data gap that is likely important to fill for transportation policy planning and analysis. Periodic reviews by BTS of existing transportation data systems, assessed against BTS's vision of user requirements, can identify data gaps and opportunities for data linkages that are important to address in order to serve priority data needs.

APPENDIX
G
Biographical Sketches

JANET L. NORWOOD (*Chair*) is a senior fellow at the Urban Institute and author of *Organizing to Count: Change in the Federal Statistical System* (1995). Previously she served as commissioner of labor statistics in the U.S. Department of Labor. She has written articles and monographs on statistical policy and on unemployment, price, and wage statistics and has testified often on these issues before congressional committees. She has been a member of the Committee on National Statistics of the National Research Council since 1991, is chair of the Advisory Committee for the Leading Indicators, and is a member of advisory committees at the National Science Foundation, at several statistical agencies, and at universities. She has a B.A. degree from Rutgers University and M.A. and Ph.D. degrees from the Fletcher School of Law and Diplomacy of Tufts University. She has received honorary LL.D. degrees from Florida International and Carnegie Mellon Universities.

VINCENT P. BARABBA is the general manager of Corporate Strategy and Knowledge Development at General Motors. He is responsible for overseeing the Business Decision Support Center and Knowledge Network Development and Integration, as well as Corporate Strategic Planning. Previously, he was the director of market intelligence for the Eastman Kodak Company, and he twice served as director of the Bureau of the Census, in the U.S. Department of Commerce. He is the past president and a fellow of the American Statistical Association and has served as U.S. representative to the population commission of the United Nations and chair of the National Research Council panel to review the statistical program of the National Center for Education Statistics. He has a B.A. degree from California State University at Northridge and an M.B.A. degree in marketing from the University of California at Los Angeles.

JAMES T. BONNEN is professor of agricultural economics at Michigan State University. His current research interests include information systems theory, the design and management of statistically based policy decision systems, and agricultural research policy. In 1981 he received the American Statistical Association's Washington Statistical Society's Julius Shiskin award for outstanding achievement in economic statistics. He is a fellow of the American Agricultural Economics Association, the American Statistical Association, and the American Association for the Advancement of Science. He has a B.A. degree from Texas A&M University, an M.A. degree from Duke University, and a Ph.D. degree from Harvard University, all in economics.

CAROL S. CARSON is the director of the Statistics Department at the International Monetary Fund. Previously she was with the Bureau of Economic Analysis, U.S. Department of Commerce, where her positions included chief economist, deputy director, and director. She teaches a graduate course in economic accounting at the George Washington University. She serves on the executive committee of the Conference on Research in Income and Wealth and on the board of directors of the National Association of Business Economists, and she was awarded the presidential rank of distinguished executive and the Shiskin Award in economic statistics. She has a B.A. degree from the College of Wooster, an M.A. degree from the Fletcher School of Law and Diplomacy at Tufts University, and a Ph.D. degree from the George Washington University.

CONSTANCE F. CITRO (*Study Director*) is a member of the senior staff of the Committee on National Statistics. She is a former vice president and deputy director of Mathematica Policy Research, Inc., and was an American Statistical Association/National Science Foundation research fellow at the Bureau of the Census. Her research has focused on the usefulness and accessibility of large, complex microdata files, as well as analysis related to income and poverty measurement. For the Committee on National Statistics, she has served as study director for several panels, including the Panel on Poverty and Family Assistance, the Panel on Retirement Income Modeling, the Panel to Evaluate the Survey of Income and Program Participation, and the Panel on Decennial Census Methodology. She is a fellow of the American Statistical Association. She has a B.A. degree from the University of Rochester and M.A. and Ph.D. degrees in political science from Yale University.

WILLIAM F. EDDY is professor of statistics at Carnegie Mellon University. His research concentrates on the computational and graphical aspects of statistics. He is particularly interested in dynamic graphics for the analysis and presentation of data, especially those dynamic graphical displays that cannot be rendered interactively. He is a fellow of the American Association for the Advancement of Science, the American Statistical Association, the Institute of Mathematical Statistics, and the Royal Statistical Society and is an elected member of the International Statistical Institute. He was the founding co-editor of *Chance* magazine and is the founding editor of the *Journal of Computational and Graphical Statistics*. He has an A.B. degree from Princeton University, and M.A., M.Phil., and Ph.D. degrees from Yale University.

EMERSON J. ELLIOTT is a consultant on education policy, federal statistics, and management. Currently his work is primarily with the National Council for Accreditation of Teacher Education and concerns development of performance standards for the content portion of teacher education in the accreditation process. Previously he headed the National Center for Education Statistics and served as the first commissioner of education statistics when the post became a presidentially appointed, Senate-confirmed position. In total he was employed by the federal government for more than 38 years in the U.S. Departments of Education and Health, Education, and Welfare, the Office of Management and Budget, and the Bureau of the Budget. He is a member of the advisory committee on research and development for the College Board. He is a member of the American Educational Research Association and a fellow of the American Statistical Association. He has a B.A. degree from Albion College and an M.A. degree in public administration from the University of Michigan.

FRANCIS B. FRANCOIS is executive director of the American Association of State Highway and Transportation Officials (AASHTO). Previously he was a member of the County Council of Prince George's County, Maryland, an elected position in which he dealt with transportation, public works, environmental, and community development issues. During his 18 years as an elected county official, he served as president of the National Association of Counties and president of the National Association of Regional Councils. He is also a registered patent attorney who engaged actively in a patent and trademark law practice before coming to AASHTO. He is a member of the board of directors and past chair of ITS America; he also serves as an ex officio member of the executive committee of the Transportation Research Board and on the boards of several other national and international transportation organizations. He has an engineering degree from Iowa State University and a J.D. degree from George Washington University.

ROBERT M. GROVES is director of the Joint Program in Survey Methodology, based at the University of Maryland. It is a National Science Foundation-sponsored consortium of the University of Maryland, the University of Michigan, and Westat, Inc. He is a professor of sociology at the University of Michigan and a research scientist at its Institute for Social Research. At the Michigan Survey Research Center, he is a member of the Survey Methodology Research Program. While on loan from the University of Michigan, he spent two years as an associate director of the Bureau of the Census. His current research interests focus on theory-building in survey participation and models of nonresponse reduction and adjustment. He has investigated the impact of alternative telephone sample designs on precision, the effect of data collection mode on the quality of survey reports, causes and remedies for nonresponse errors in surveys, estimation and explanation of interviewer variance in survey responses, and other topics in survey methods. He has a B.A. degree from Dartmouth College and a Ph.D.from the University of Michigan.

NANCY HUMPHREY is a senior staff officer at the Transportation Research Board (TRB), a unit of the National Research Council. She has been with the Studies and Information Services Division of TRB for more than 10 years and has managed several policy studies, including a review of transportation data needs for national decision making—*Special Report 234: Data for Decisions*—that recommended creation of the Bureau of Transportation Statistics. She has an M.A. degree in public and private management from the Yale School of Management.

ROBERT E. MARTINEZ is the secretary of transportation in the Commonwealth of Virginia. He is charged with oversight of the development and implementation of Virginia's transportation program. He has management and budgetary responsibility for the commonwealth's Department of Transportation, Department of Motor Vehicles, Department of Aviation, Department of Rail and Public Transportation, and the Virginia Port Authority. He also serves as chairman of the Commonwealth Transportation Board, which oversees highway construction, highway use regulations, compliance with federal transportation laws, and administration of the Transportation Trust Fund and the Highway Maintenance and Operating Fund. Previously he was manager of strategic planning at Norfolk Southern Corporation, focusing primarily on intermodal projects and transportation planning. He has also worked for the federal government in the U.S. Department of Transportation. He was deputy administrator of the Maritime Administration and was later appointed as associate deputy secretary of transportation and director of the Office of Intermodalism. He has a B.A. degree from Columbia University and an M.A. degree in international relations and a Ph.D. degree in political science from Yale University.

MICHAEL D. MEYER is professor of civil and environmental engineering, director of the Transportation Research and Education Center, and chair of the School of Civil and Environmental Engineering at the Georgia Institute of Technology. Previously he was director of transportation planning and development for Massachusetts, where he was responsible for statewide planning, project development, traffic engineering, and transportation research. He is an active member of numerous professional organizations and has chaired committees relating to public transportation, transportation planning, environmental impact analysis, transportation policy, transportation education, and intermodal transportation. He has a B.S. degree from the University of Wisconsin, an M.S. degree from Northwestern University, and a Ph.D. degree from the Massachusetts Institute of Technology, all in civil engineering.

PETER L. SZANTON is president of Szanton Associates and a consultant on strategic planning and organizational renewal. An associate director of the U.S. Office of Management and Budget during the Carter administration, he also served with two presidential commissions on federal organization and was founding president of the New York City RAND Institute. He is the author of reports and articles on a number of subjects and of books on national service, federal organization, and the relationships between consultants and municipal officials. He serves on the boards of several nonprofit organizations and chairs the board of the National Academy of Public Administration. He has B.A., M.A., and Ph.D. degrees from Harvard University.

GERALDINE A. TURNER is chief economist with Virginia's Department of Motor Vehicles. Previously she served as senior economist with the Virginia Department of Taxation and associate legislative analyst with the Joint Legislative Audit and Review Commission. In 1989 she was coordinator for Virginia's Tax Amnesty program. She has B.S. and M.A. degrees from Virginia Commonwealth University, both in economics.

CHARLES A. WAITE is a consultant in economic statistics with CBW Consulting. He is a former associate director for economic programs at the Bureau of the Census, where he directed the quinquennial economic and agriculture censuses, as well as preparation of such principal economic indicators as retail sales and foreign merchandise trade. Prior to that he served as chief economist and associate director at the U.S. Department of Commerce's Bureau of Economic Analysis, where he was closely involved in the calculation and analysis of the National Income and Product Accounts and the system of leading economic indicators. He is a fellow of the National Association of Business Economists. He has a B.A. degree from the University of Michigan and pursued graduate studies in economics at Michigan State University and the American University.

ALICE J. WATLAND is senior program officer for transportation data at the Transportation Research Board, a unit of the National Research Council, where she coordinates the activities of the standing committees that address national, state, and local transportation data policy issues. Previously she worked with the National Association of Regional Councils and Mid-America Regional Council, the Metropolitan Planning Organization in Kansas City, Missouri, in areas of economic development. She has a B.A. degree from North Dakota State University and an M.A. degree in research methods and statistics from the University of Missouri-Kansas City.

JULIAN WOLPERT is professor of geography, public affairs, and urban planning at Princeton University's Woodrow Wilson School, where he chairs the program in urban and regional planning. His research interests include land use and transportation planning and the provision of urban public services. He is a member of the National Academy of Sciences and previously chaired the Commission on Behavioral and Social Sciences and Education, served on the executive committee of the Transportation Research Board, and served on other NAS-NRC commissions and panels. He has a B.A. degree from Columbia University and M.S. and Ph.D. degrees from the University of Wisconsin.